Third Edition

Guide to Parallel Programming

on Sequent Computer Systems

PRENTICE HALL
Englewood Cliffs, New Jersey 07632

Editorial/production supervision: MARY P. ROTTINO
Manufacturing buyer: MARY ELIZABETH MCCARTNEY
Prepress buyer: SUSAN BRUNKE
Acquisitions editor: GREGORY G. DOENCH
Editorial assistant: JOAN MAGRABI

1 1 8 1 4 2 7

Published by Prentice-Hall, Inc.
A Simon & Schuster Company
Englewood Cliffs, New Jersey 07632

The publisher offers discounts on this book when ordered
in bulk quantities. For more information, write:

> Special Sales/Professional Marketing
> Professional & Technical Reference Division
> Prentice Hall
> Englewood Cliffs, New Jersey 07632

Sequent, Symmetry, DYNIX, and Balance are registered trademarks of Sequent Computer Systems, Inc.
DYNIX/ptx is a trademark of Sequent Computer Systems, Inc.
386 and 486 are trademarks of Intel Corporation.
POSIX is a trademark of the Institute of Electrical and Electronic Engineers, Inc.
UNIX is a registered trademark of AT&T.

Printed in the United States of America
10 9 8 7 6 5 4 3 2 1

ISBN 0-13-370776-8

Prentice-Hall International (UK) Limited, *London*
Prentice-Hall of Australia Pty. Limited, *Sydney*
Prentice-Hall Canada Inc., *Toronto*
Prentice-Hall Hispanoamericana, S.A., *Mexico*
Prentice-Hall of India Private Limited, *New Delhi*
Prentice-Hall of Japan, Inc., *Tokyo*
Simon & Schuster Asia Pte. Ltd., *Singapore*
Editora Prentice-Hall do Brasil, Ltda., *Rio de Janeiro*

17/4/97

Acknowledgements

The authors wish to thank all the people who contributed their time, expertise, and encouragement in the development of this book.

Learning Resources
Centre

Contents

About This Guide

Figures

Tables

About This Guide

Overview

This guide introduces the basic concepts of parallel programming. After reading this guide, you should be able to develop parallel programs that execute on a Sequent Symmetry system running either the DYNIX/ptx or the DYNIX operating system.

Both operating systems support parallel programming; however, this version of the *Guide to Parallel Programming* focuses on parallel programming on a Symmetry system running DYNIX/ptx. Most of the information in this *Guide* can also be applied to parallel programming on a Symmetry system running the DYNIX operating system. For a description of the differences between the DYNIX and the DYNIX/ptx operating systems that affect parallel programming and the exact commands required to compile and execute a parallel program using these resources, refer to Appendix C of this guide.

Assumptions About the Reader

This guide assumes that you have experience writing, executing, and debugging C, C++, Pascal, or FORTRAN programs. This manual also assumes that you are familiar with the UNIX process model. (For a reference on this topic, see the "Related Publications" section at the end of this preface.)

When developing parallel programs for a Sequent Symmetry system, you should have access to the manuals for that operating system, especially the manual that describes the standard commands, system calls, and subroutine libraries provided with the operating system. For DYNIX/ptx systems, this manual is the *DYNIX/ptx Reference Manual*; for DYNIX systems, this is the *DYNIX Programmer's Manual*.

Organization

Chapters 1 and 2 of this manual contain introductory information about parallel programming and the Sequent Symmetry architecture. Chapter 3 describes some of the parallel programming tools that are available for use on Sequent Symmetry systems.

If you are a FORTRAN programmer, you should read Chapters 1–6 before attempting to write a parallel program. Chapter 4 explains how to use the FORTRAN parallel-programming directives to execute DO-loop iterations in parallel. Chapters 5 and 6 describe how to use the parallel-programming library to execute subroutines in parallel. While reading Chapters 4 and 5, you may want to refer to Appendix A, which includes complete listings of parallel programs written in FORTRAN.

If you are a C, C++, or Pascal programmer, you should read Chapters 1–3, skip Chapter 4, and then read Chapters 5 and 6 before attempting to write a parallel program. Chapters 5 and 6 describe how to use the parallel-programming library to execute subroutines in parallel. While reading Chapters 5 and 6, you may want to refer to Appendix A, which includes listings of parallel programs written in C, C++, and Pascal.

For your convenience, Appendix B lists the DYNIX/ptx man pages for the parallel-programming library.

For information about more advanced techniques, read Chapter 7. If you are interested in designing your own parallel-programming support package, read Chapter 8.

If you are a DYNIX user, you should review Appendix C, which describes the differences between the DYNIX/ptx and DYNIX operating systems that affect parallel programming.

For more information on a specific topic, refer to Appendix D, which contains a bibliography of current literature on parallel-programming topics.

Notation

The following conventions are used throughout this manual:

bold	Shell commands and options are shown in **bold** type and must be entered exactly as shown. System calls and routine names are also shown in **bold** type.
italic	Filenames and values that you must replace are shown in *italic* type. *Italics* are also used for emphasis and to identify new terms.
`constant width`	Program listings are shown in constant-width font.

Related Publications

For more information about the UNIX operating system, refer to the following document:

- *The Design of the UNIX Operating System*, by Maurice J. Bach (Prentice-Hall, Inc., Englewood Cliffs, New Jersey: 1986)

This book contains an excellent introduction to the UNIX process model.

The following Sequent documents supplement this manual:

For DYNIX/ptx:

- The *Symmetry Multiprocessor Architecture Overview* contains information about the Symmetry system architecture.

- The *DYNIX/ptx Reference Manual* and the *DYNIX/ptx C and Language Tools* binder contain man pages for all of the system calls and routines referenced in this book.

- The *DYNIX/ptx C User's Manual* describes the Sequent extensions to the C language that support parallel programming.

- The *ptx/FORTRAN User's Manual* provides a detailed description of the ptx/FORTRAN language, the compiler and its options, and the parallel programming directives.

- The *ptx/C++ Release Notes* as well as AT&T's *C++ Product Reference Manual* and *Library Manual* provide information on the C++ translator and its options.

- The *ptx/PASCAL Release Notes* describes how to invoke and use the ptx/PASCAL compiler. The *EPC Pascal-E User's Manual* provides a detailed description of the Pascal language.

For DYNIX:

- The *Symmetry Multiprocessor Architecture Overview* contains information about the Symmetry system architecture.

- The *DYNIX Programmer's Manual* contains man pages for all system calls and routines.

- The *ATS C User's Manual* describes the Sequent extensions to the C language that support parallel programming.

- The *ATS FORTRAN User's Manual* provides a detailed description of the ATS FORTRAN language, the compiler and its options, and the parallel-programming directives.

- The *DYNIX C++ Translator Release Notes* as well as AT&T's *C++ Product Reference Manual* and *Library Manual* provide information on the C++ translator and its options.

- The *Sequent Pascal Compiler User's Manual* describes how to invoke and use the Pascal compiler on DYNIX.

Chapter 1

Parallel Programming and the Sequent Symmetry System

Chapter 1
Parallel Programming and the Sequent Symmetry System

1.1 Introduction

This chapter introduces the Sequent Symmetry system architecture and discusses the parallel programming capabilities of the system.

1.2 Sequent Symmetry Systems

Most Symmetry systems are multiprocessor systems that share a single common memory. *Multiprocessors* are computers that incorporate multiple identical processors (CPUs). Symmetry CPUs are general-purpose, 32-bit microprocessors. The following characteristics distinguish the Symmetry architecture from other parallel architectures:

- **True multiprocessor.** Sequent Symmetry systems are true multiprocessors, not array (vector) processors.

- **Tightly coupled.** All processors share a single pool of memory, to enhance resource sharing and communication among different processes.

- **Symmetric.** All processors are identical, and all processors can execute both user code and kernel (operating system) code. However, some processors may contain optional floating-point hardware.

- **Common bus.** All processors, memory modules, and I/O interfaces plug into a single high-speed bus. This feature greatly simplifies the addition of processors, memory, and I/O bandwidth.

- **Transparent.** Programs written for a single-processor system can run on a Sequent Symmetry system without modification for multiprocessing support. Processors can be added or removed without modifying the operating system or user applications.

- **Dynamic load balancing.** Processors automatically schedule themselves to ensure that all processors are kept busy as long as there are executable processes (instruction streams) available. When a processor stops executing one process (because that process is finished or is waiting for an I/O operation), it begins executing the next available process in the system-wide run queue.

- **Hardware support for mutual exclusion.** To support exclusive access to shared data structures, the system includes a user-accessible hardware locking mechanism.

- **Coherent cache.** Automatic mechanisms ensure data integrity for shared variables in all processes, regardless of the processor on which a process executes.

The Symmetry is an Intel x86-based machine that, on most models, runs both the DYNIX and the DYNIX/ptx operating systems. The DYNIX operating system is a version of UNIX 4.2BSD that also supports most of the utilities, libraries, and system calls provided by UNIX System V. DYNIX/ptx is Sequent's POSIX-compliant implementation of System V.

Both operating systems support parallel programming; however, this version of the *Guide to Parallel Programming* focuses on parallel programming on a Symmetry system running DYNIX/ptx. Most of the information in this guide can also be applied to parallel programming on a Symmetry system running the DYNIX operating system; but, for a more accurate description of the resources available under DYNIX and the exact commands required to compile and execute a parallel program using these resources, you should refer to Appendix C of this guide.

Table 1-1 compares the various Symmetry systems. For additional
configuration information, refer to the *Symmetry Multiprocessor Architecture
Overview* and the *S3 System Summary*.

Table 1-1
System Configurations

Model	No. of Processors	Processor Type	Floating-point Accelerator	Memory (megabytes)
S3	1 only	Intel 386	none	8 to 40
S16	2 to 6	Intel 386	optional	8 to 80
S27	2 to 10	Intel 386	optional	8 to 128
S81	2 to 30	Intel 386	optional	8 to 384
S2000/40	1 only	Intel 486	none	8 to 64
S2000/200	2 to 6	Intel 486	none	8 to 128
S2000/400	2 to 10	Intel 486	none	8 to 128
S2000/700	2 to 30	Intel 486	none	8 to 384

Every Symmetry system provides 256 megabytes of virtual address space per
process.

For secondary mass storage, Sequent Symmetry systems offer a variety of
disk and tape drives. For information on what is available for a specific
Symmetry system, refer to the *Symmetry Multiprocessor Architecture
Overview* or the *S3 System Summary*.

1.3 Parallel Programming

Sequent Symmetry systems support the two basic kinds of parallel
programming: multiprogramming and multitasking. *Multiprogramming* is
an operating system feature that allows a computer to execute multiple
unrelated programs concurrently. (A multiuser operating system is a good
example of this.) *Multitasking* is a programming technique that allows a
single application to consist of multiple processes executing concurrently.
This manual is primarily about multitasking, since the DYNIX/ptx operating
system does multiprogramming for all user programs automatically.

Many systems offer multiprogramming and some offer multitasking, but a
Sequent Symmetry system offers these features with an important difference.
By definition, parallel programs execute *concurrently*, meaning that at any
instant, the system is in the process of executing multiple programs. On a
Sequent Symmetry system, parallel programs execute *simultaneously*: at
any instant, the system can be executing multiple instructions from multiple
processes. Thus, parallel programming on a Sequent Symmetry system has
two special benefits: multiprogramming yields improved *system throughput*
for multiple programs, and multitasking yields improved *execution speed* for
individual programs.

1.3.1 Multiprogramming on a Symmetry System

The multiuser, multiprogrammed UNIX environment adapts naturally to the
Symmetry multiprocessing architecture and automatically schedules
processes for optimal throughput. In other versions of the UNIX operating
system, executable processes wait in a run queue; when the CPU suspends or
terminates execution of one process, it switches to the process at the head of
the run queue. DYNIX/ptx uses the same technique, except that a pool of
processors is available to execute processes from the run queue. DYNIX/ptx
balances the system load among the available processors, keeping all
processors busy as long as there is enough work available, thus using the full
computing capability of each processor.

On a Symmetry system, work loads consisting of multiple, single-stream,
computation-intensive applications show a nearly linear increase in system
throughput as more processors are added. Even applications that require
significant amounts of I/O activity, such as document formatters and
compilers, show performance-per-processor curves well above those
previously thought possible, and this increase in performance is achieved
with no extra effort by the programmer.

1.3.2 Multitasking on a Symmetry System

The Symmetry system supports multitasking by allowing a single application
to consist of multiple, closely cooperating processes. You can use the system
utilities that support multitasking as well as write your own multitasking
applications.

System Utilities That Use Multitasking

The operating system automatically performs multitasking for commands that support parallel processing when the **PARALLEL** environment variable is set to a value greater than 1 or the **–P***n* option is used to specify the number of processes that will execute in parallel. The value of the **PARALLEL** environment variable or the value of *n* can be greater than the number of processors on the system, but it is limited to 256. You should use this option with discretion since the processes you create will compete for system resources with the processes generated by other users. These features are supported for jobs that run in the background only.

Commands that support these features include **sh**, **lint**, and **make**. The parallel processing support for the **make** utility, for example, allows you to indicate which objects can be built simultaneously and to use the **PARALLEL** environment variable or the **–P** option to generate multiple command streams. For more information on **make**, refer to the **make**(1) man page.

Writing Your Own Multitasking Applications

Sequent language software includes multitasking extensions to C, C++, Pascal, and FORTRAN. The DYNIX/ptx parallel-programming library includes routines to create, synchronize, and terminate parallel processes from C, C++, Pascal, and FORTRAN programs.

The speedup that can be gained by multitasking is determined by the following factors:

- The portion of the program's time that can be spent executing parallel code. This factor varies with the application, but a surprisingly large variety of applications need to spend less than 1% of their time executing sequential code.

- The number of processors available to the application (see Section 1.2). Sequent software allows you to design programs that adapt themselves to the number of processors in the system, so that the same program can run on different-sized systems without modification.

- The hardware contention imposed by multiple processors competing for the same resources, such as the system bus and system memory. On Sequent Symmetry systems, this overhead is negligible for sequential programs, since CPU memory operations access cache memory, not the system bus. The overhead for parallel programs varies significantly from one to another.

- The overhead in creating multiple processes. This overhead is measured in only hundredths of a second per process.

- The overhead in synchronization and communication among multiple processes. Because the Sequent architecture includes shared memory and hardware-based synchronization facilities, this overhead can be measured in microseconds.

The remainder of this manual explains in detail how to develop efficient multitasking programs on the Sequent system. Chapter 2 discusses parallel programming terms and concepts. Chapter 3 discusses several parallel programming models that have been implemented on Sequent Symmetry systems. Chapters 4 through 6 explain how to create parallel programs using Sequent multitasking tools.

Chapter 2
Elements of Parallel Programming

Figures

Chapter 2
Elements of Parallel Programming

2.1 Introduction

This chapter introduces some principles of parallel programming and some terms and concepts that you will need to know before designing a parallel program. Section 2.2 explains the goals of a parallel programmer and takes you through the process of identifying the parallelism in an example job. Section 2.3 describes the two basic multitasking methods: *data partitioning* and *function partitioning*. The remaining sections introduce some elements of parallel programming that are not common in sequential programming, including:

- Creation and termination of multiple processes

- Creation of shared and private data

- *Scheduling*, the division of computing tasks among parallel processes

- Interprocess communication

- Task synchronization and mutual exclusion

- I/O from parallel processes

- Signals and parallel processes

2.2 Programming Goals

In adapting an application for multitasking, you will have the following goals:

- Run as much of the program in parallel as possible.

- Balance the computational load as evenly as possible among parallel processes.

The extent to which you meet these goals ultimately determines the execution speed of the program.

To help illustrate the importance of these goals, imagine an automobile repair shop with four equally skilled repair people, Joe, Gary, Dave, and Sue. If Joe can change the tires on a car in two hours, the four repair people should be able to change the four tires in a half hour, right? Not necessarily. Let's look at the tasks involved in changing a tire:

1. Fill out the paperwork while the customer describes the work to be done. **(10 minutes)**

2. Get the new tires out of stock. **(10 minutes or 5 minutes/pair)**

3. Drive the car into the shop and raise it on a hydraulic lift. **(10 minutes)**

4. Change the four tires. **(15 minutes/tire)**

5. Lower the hydraulic lift and drive the car out of the garage. **(10 minutes)**

6. Discard the old tires. **(10 minutes or 5 minutes/pair)**

7. Prepare the bill and charge the customer. **(10 minutes)**

Clearly, the four repair people could change the tires at the same time, leaving the paperwork and miscellaneous jobs to Joe. If we chart the shop activities based on this assumption, the job takes 1 hour and 15 minutes, as illustrated in Figure 2-1.

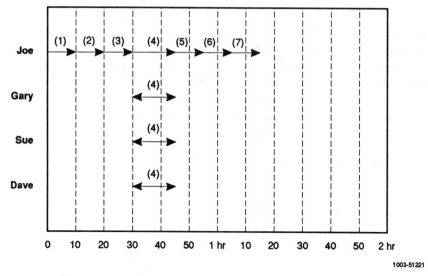

Figure 2-1. Changing tires: parallel approach.

Notice, however, that with this approach, three of the repair people are doing nothing for an hour each: the work load is not well-balanced. There are three person-hours of idle time and the job is completed only 45 minutes sooner than when Joe does the whole job himself.

Let's try another approach and see if we can better meet the multitasking goals: to balance the work load and do as much of the job in parallel as possible. Maybe we can shorten the job and eliminate some waste by having Gary, Dave, and Sue handle more tasks in parallel with Joe.

Let's say that after talking with the customer for five minutes, Joe knows what kind of tires the customer wants. He could send both Gary and Sue to get a pair of tires while he completes arrangements with the customer. Dave is still idle, so Joe could send Dave to put the car on the hydraulic lift. (Naturally, Joe has to take a little time to explain what he wants the others to do, but for now let's assume that the time is negligible.) At this point, Joe finishes the paperwork and Gary and Sue arrive with the new tires. However, Dave is still putting the car on the lift. Joe, Gary, and Sue must wait for Dave. Here the job has an inherent *order dependency*, a point where a task depends on the result of a previous task and cannot proceed until the previous task is finished. (Section 2.7 explains more about order dependencies.)

Once the car is on the lift, the four repair people can change the tires in parallel. After the tires are changed, Joe can finish the paperwork and charge the customer. At the same time, Gary and Sue can discard the old tires and Dave can lower the car and drive it out of the shop. Figure 2-2 illustrates this task sequence.

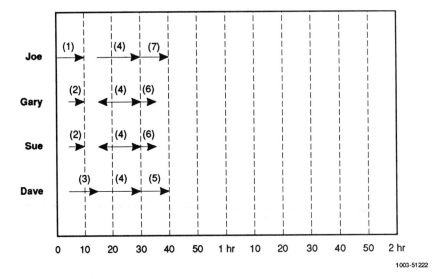

Figure 2-2. Changing tires: balanced parallel approach.

The repair people are now doing as many tasks in parallel as the job allows, and the work load is distributed as evenly as possible. The total job takes only 40 minutes. (Notice that this is very close to the original guess; that is, that four people could do the job in 30 minutes.) The repair people collectively have only 40 minutes of idle time, and this task sequence is 1 hour and 20 minutes faster than when Joe did the whole job himself.

Adapting an application for multitasking is very much like scheduling work in Joe's auto shop. Almost every application has certain inherent dependencies that prohibit completely parallel execution. However, you can achieve the shortest possible execution time by executing as many tasks in parallel as possible and by balancing the work load. In a surprising number of applications, you will find that a large percentage of the computation required can be done in parallel.

2.3 Programming Methods: Data- and Function-Partitioning

The first step in adapting an application for efficient multitasking is to choose the right programming method. Most applications naturally lend themselves to one of two multitasking programming methods: *data partitioning* or *function partitioning*.

Data partitioning involves creating multiple, *identical* processes and assigning a portion of the data to each process. (This method is sometimes called *homogeneous multitasking*, because it involves identical tasks executed in parallel.) Data partitioning is appropriate for applications that perform the same operations repeatedly on large collections of data. In the auto shop example, fetching tires in parallel and changing tires in parallel are examples of data partitioning. In programming terms, data partitioning is appropriate for applications that require loops to perform calculations on arrays or matrices: data partitioning is done by executing the loop iterations in parallel. Algorithms such as matrix multiplication or Fourier transformations and applications such as ray tracing or signal processing adapt well to data partitioning.

Function partitioning, on the other hand, involves creating multiple *unique* processes with each process simultaneously performing different operations on a shared data set. (This method is sometimes called *heterogeneous multitasking*, because it involves different tasks executed in parallel.) Function partitioning is suitable for applications which must perform many different operations on the same data. In programming terms, function partitioning is appropriate for applications that include many unique subroutines or functions. Applications such as flight simulation, program compilation, and traditional process control adapt well to function partitioning.

While some applications require function partitioning, and some applications lend themselves to a combination of these methods, most applications adapt most easily to data partitioning. While both programming methods can be effective, the data partitioning method offers the following advantages over function partitioning:

- Work loads are easy to balance among processors.

- Minimal programming effort is required.

- Programs adapt automatically to the number of processors in a system.

2.4 Process Creation and Termination

Process creation is analogous to hiring repair people for Joe's auto shop, and similar considerations apply. Joe needs enough employees to get work done quickly, but he has to pay them even when there is no work for them to do. Therefore, Joe wants only as many employees as he can keep busy most of the time. A parallel programmer has to make the same tradeoffs, only instead of employees the programmer has UNIX processes. Each task can be executed by a different process or the same task can execute on different data, but all processes execute concurrently. The programmer needs enough processes to execute a program quickly, but not so many that they are often sitting idle and consuming CPU cycles, waiting for work.

Creating Sequential Processes

In DYNIX/ptx, as in other UNIX-based operating systems, a new process is created by using the **fork**() system call. The new (or *child*) process is a duplicate copy of the old (or *parent*) process, with the same data, register contents, and program counter. If the parent has files open, the child has access to the same files. So that the parent and child know which process is which, a *process identification number* (process ID) is returned to each. When a child process is created, the process ID number 0 is returned to the child, and the child's process ID number is returned to the parent. From this point on, the parent and child are separate entities.

Creating Parallel Processes

Depending on the programming model you use for an application, you can use either the **fork**() system call or the **m_fork**() routine in your parallel programs, but not both. The **m_fork**() routine is used for both data- and function-partitioning applications while the **fork**() system call is typically used in function-partitioning applications only. Calling **m_fork**() causes a switch to a shared stack before execution of the main program. The **m_fork**() routine then initializes shared memory and ensures that variables declared with keywords such as `shared` and `private` in C are mapped to the appropriate memory area. As with **fork**(), a child process is a duplicate of the parent process (except for process ID). Thus, if the parent process has access to shared memory, so does the child process. Refer to Chapter 8 for more information on shared memory mapping.

In contrast, if you use the **fork()** system call in your parallel program, you must manually set up a communication mechanism (**fork()** uses a private stack). You can't fork on a shared stack because the routines which control access to shared memory are not part of the kernel.

Since a UNIX fork operation is relatively expensive, a parallel application typically forks (by means of **fork()** or **m_fork()**) as many processes as it is likely to need at the beginning of the program, and does not terminate any process until the program is completed. If a process is not needed during certain code sequences, the process can wait in a busy loop (spin) or relinquish the processor until it is needed. (The cost to an existing process of relinquishing a processor and later reacquiring it is rather low, while the cost of spinning can be very high in terms of system throughput.)

2.5 Shared and Local Data

Typically, multitasking programs include both shared and local data. Shared data is accessible by both parent and child processes and is stored in shared memory. Local data is accessible by only one process and is stored in private memory. In the "Joe's garage" example, the car might be considered shared data, since it was accessible to all the repair people, and the tires might be considered local data, because each repair person worked with his or her own tire.

There are several advantages to sharing data:

- It uses less memory than having multiple copies.

- It avoids the overhead of making copies of the data for each process.

- Most important, it provides a simple and efficient mechanism for communication between processes.

On a Symmetry system, each process has 256 megabytes of virtual memory. This memory space contains the process's *text* (program source) area, its private data area, and its private stack, as illustrated in Figure 2-3. Program text is read from the program's executable file. The initialized portion of the private data area is also read from the program's executable file and then mapped into memory. A program may expand its private data area to a fixed address using the **brk()** system call or by an incremental number of bytes using the **sbrk()** system call. The portion of the data area that is allocated at run time is called the *heap*. You can use the C library routines **malloc()** and **free()** in your program to manage the size of the heap.

The stack area is automatically created by the kernel at run time. Adjusting the size of the stack is unnecessary because its size is dynamically adjusted by the kernel.

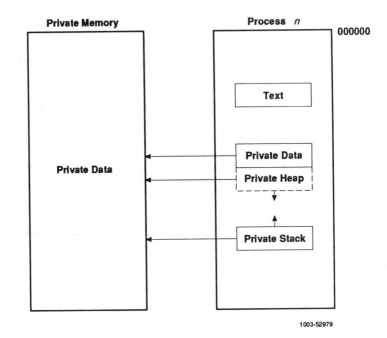

Figure 2-3.   Virtual memory: sequential process.

If the program includes any shared data, the process's virtual memory space also contains a shared data area and a shared heap. If the program calls routines in the DYNIX/ptx Parallel Programming Library (either the **–mp** or **–lpps** option was specified at compile time), it may also contain a shared stack. Figure 2-4 illustrates the virtual memory contents of a parallel process.

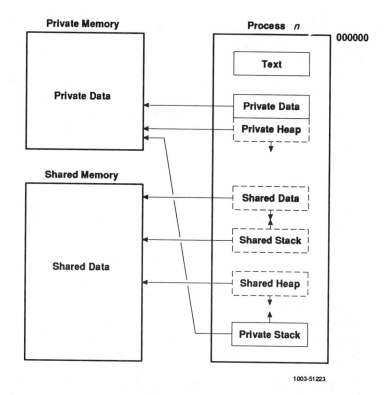

Figure 2-4. Virtual memory: parallel process.

Notice that as memory is allocated, the heaps grow from lower memory addresses to higher ones, while the stacks grow in the opposite direction. The value of **_priv_stack_limit** and **_stack_limit** determine how large the private stack and the shared stack, respectively, can grow. In the case of the shared heap and the private stack, the **_priv_stack_limit** variable acts as both an upper bound for the stack and a lower bound for the heap. You can display the default value of both **_stack_limit** and **_priv_stack_limit** from your program. If necessary, you can then assign new values to these limits, but the values you assign should be consistent with your application's memory layout. For example, adding the following statement to your program sets the limit for the shared stack to one megabyte (100000_{16}):

```
int _stack_limit = 0x100000;
```

If the process forks any child processes, each child process inherits access to the parent's shared memory area and shared stack. Both the parent and children then have access to the shared data.

The DYNIX/ptx C compiler, as well as the ptx/C++, ptx/PASCAL, and ptx/FORTRAN compilers, includes mechanisms to designate data as shared or local to a process. Chapters 4, 5, and 6 explain how to use these mechanisms to allocate shared and private memory for data-partitioning and function-partitioning applications.

2.6 Scheduling Algorithms

In multitasking programs, tasks can be scheduled among processes using three types of algorithms: prescheduling, static scheduling, or dynamic scheduling.

Prescheduling

In prescheduling, the task division is determined by the programmer before the program is compiled. Prescheduled programs cannot automatically balance the computing load according to the data or the number of CPUs in the system. Therefore, this method is appropriate only for function-partitioning applications, where each process is performing a different task. To schedule, the programmer assigns a specific task to each processor. For example, one processor may be responsible for handling signals from input devices, and another processor may be responsible for updating a graphics frame buffer.

Static Scheduling

In static scheduling, the tasks are scheduled by the processes at run time, but the work is divided in some predetermined way. The static-scheduling algorithm for a process is:

1. Figure out which tasks I will do.

2. Do all my tasks.

3. Wait until all other processes finish their tasks.

For example, your program might include a 100-iteration loop. Using static scheduling, if your program uses 10 processes, each process might execute 10 iterations of the loop.

Dynamic Scheduling

In dynamic scheduling, each process checks for tasks at run time by examining a task queue or a "do-me-next" array index. The dynamic-scheduling algorithm for a process is:

1. Wait until some tasks appear.

2. Remove the first task from the list and do it.

3. If there are any more tasks, go to step 2. Otherwise, go to step 1.

For example, a dynamically scheduled program might perform a matrix multiplication, with each process computing three matrix elements and then returning for more until all the work is done.

Dynamic scheduling provides dynamic load balancing: all processes keep working as long as there is work to be done. Since the work load is evenly distributed among the processes, the work can be completed sooner. Static scheduling produces static load balancing: since the division of tasks is statically determined, several processors may stand idle while one processor completes its share of the job. However, dynamic scheduling entails more overhead than static scheduling. Each time a process schedules another task for itself, it must check the shared queue to make sure there is work to do, and it must remove that task from the queue. Generally, though, unless each task is to work on a very small amount of data, or you know in advance that static scheduling is efficient for your application, it is best to use dynamic scheduling.

Static and dynamic scheduling are most easily achieved with homogeneous multitasking algorithms. However, dynamic scheduling is also possible with heterogeneous tasks, as evidenced by the DYNIX/ptx operating system itself. For more information on this topic, refer to the article "Guided Self-Scheduling: A Practical Scheduling Scheme for Parallel Supercomputers" by C.D. Polychronopoulos (see *Bibliography*).

NOTE

It is up to the user to provide a priority mechanism to schedule parallel programs. Whenever the number of processes exceeds the number of processors, performance degrades significantly because programs are waiting in a spin-loop for a process that has possibly been preempted.

2.7 Program Dependence

To create a parallel version of a program, you must identify the dependencies in your sequential program. To do this, you must understand program dependence theory. *Program dependence* defines how, in order to guarantee correct results, some program operations *depend* on previous operations, while some may be executed in any order. When you have defined every program dependence for a specified program unit, you have identified all the ordering necessary to guarantee correct results.

When a program unit has no dependencies, the statements can be executed in any order, including simultaneously. In the following example, statements 2 and 3 are completely independent and can be executed in any order *after* statement 1 is executed:

```
1   A = B + C
2   D = A * 5
3   E = A + 6
```

There are two classes of program dependence: data dependence and control dependence. These are described in the following sections.

Data Dependence. There are three types of data dependence. The first and most familiar is called *flow dependence* or *true dependence*. It occurs when one operation sets a data value that is used by ("flows to") a subsequent operation. In the previous example, the value A is set in statement 1 and used in both statements 2 and 3.

The second type of data dependence, *antidependence*, occurs when one operation *reads* a memory location that is written by a subsequent operation. In the following example, statement 1 must be executed before statement 2, because statement 1 uses the current value of C.

```
1   A = B + C
2   C = B * 5.
3   A = D - 6.
```

The final type of data dependence, *output dependence*, occurs when one operation *writes* a value in a memory location and that same memory location is used to write a value in a subsequent operation. In the previous example statement 3 must be executed after statement 1, or A will contain the wrong data value at the end of this program segment.

NOTE

For more information on thee theory of data dependence, refer to the article "Advanced Compiler Optimization for Supercomputers," *by Padua and Wolfe (see Bibliography).*

Control Dependence. The other category of program dependence is called *control dependence*. This category includes dependencies that are due to the required flow of control in a program. In the following example, the execution of statement 2 depends on the result of the test in statement 1.

```
1    IF ( X .GT. 0)
2        A = B + 5.
```

If you can identify all the program dependencies within a program unit, you can determine the set of synchronization points and mechanisms required to transform a given program, loop, or subroutine to run correctly in parallel. Process synchronization is discussed in the following section, and some special mechanisms for use in synchronizing parallel FORTRAN loops are discussed in Chapter 4. Chapter 7 describes code optimizations which can minimize the number of synchronizations required, thus reducing the overhead for a parallel program while preserving the correctness of the code.

The previous examples were all in FORTRAN, but the principles described can be extended to other languages, looping code segments, and different program units such as subroutines or procedures. These program dependencies can be discovered and transformed manually, or by a preprocessor such as KAP/Sequent, or both. Chapter 3 provides a detailed description of KAP/Sequent. Chapter 4 gives detailed instructions for manually identifying the dependencies needed to correctly parallelize a large percentage of FORTRAN loops.

In the future, there will be increasing emphasis on the use of automatic parallelizing tools. For now it is sufficient to recognize that all real application programs contain program dependencies, and that synchronization mechanisms can be used to ensure correct parallel execution of these programs.

2.8 Process Synchronization

To ensure that a process does not read the value of a shared-memory variable before another process has written that value, parallel processes must be synchronized. A common synchronization method is a semaphore. On Sequent Symmetry systems, a *semaphore* is defined as a shared data structure that is used to synchronize the actions of multiple cooperating processes. The simplest type of semaphore in a Symmetry system (and the semaphore upon which all others can be based) is a lock (also called a spin lock).

2.8.1 Locks

A lock ensures that only one process at a time can access a shared data structure. A lock has two values: locked and unlocked. Before attempting to access a shared data structure, a process waits until the lock associated with the data structure is unlocked, indicating that no other process is accessing the data structure. The process then locks the lock, accesses the data structure, and unlocks the lock. While a process is waiting for a lock to become unlocked, it *spins* by running a loop that does nothing except check on the availability of the lock—hence the name "spin lock." Spinning prevents the overhead and delay involved in relinquishing the CPU if the lock will be available soon. This spinning is also referred to as a *busy wait*.

The locking mechanisms provided on Symmetry systems perform the actions required to acquire a lock (see that it is unlocked; then relock it) as a single indivisible operation. Hence it is impossible for two processes to acquire a lock at the same time, and the locking operations are very fast because there is no operating system intervention.

A *critical section* begins with a lock operation and ends with an unlock operation. Figure 2-5 illustrates how a lock is used to prevent multiple processes from executing a dependent section simultaneously.

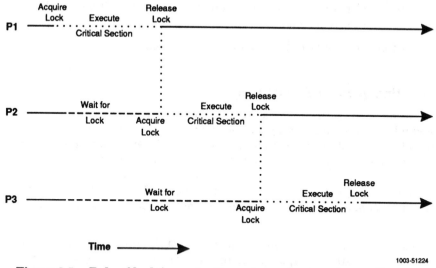

1003-51224

Figure 2-5. Role of lock in protecting a dependent section. This figure illustrates what happens when three processors try to enter a dependent section simultaneously. All processors attempt to acquire the lock immediately, but only P1 succeeds: P2 and P3 must wait while P1 executes the critical section. When P1 releases the lock, P2 and P3 again attempt to acquire it, and P2 wins: P3 must wait again.

2.8.2 Ordering and Counting/Queuing Semaphores

Semaphores other than locks can be used to protect dependent sections and manage queues.

Ordering Semaphores

Ordering semaphores are used to ensure that *order-dependent* code sections are executed in the proper order. To do this, you create a semaphore, N, to indicate how many times the dependent section has been executed. The algorithm for a process using the semaphore is:

1. Figure out which iteration of the dependent section to execute next.

2. If N equals the iteration number, execute the dependent section.

3. If N does not equal the iteration number, spin until it does and then execute the dependent section.

4. After executing the dependent section, increment N.

Counting/Queuing Semaphores

Counting/queuing semaphores are useful for queue management. When several processes are waiting for a lock, the lock goes to the first process that tries to acquire it after it is unlocked. Counting/queuing semaphores can ensure that the lock is assigned instead to the process that has waited the longest for it. This type of semaphore is also useful for managing several instances of a given resource (such as message buffers). In these situations, the value N of a counting/queuing semaphore can be interpreted as follows:

$N > 0$ N is the number of instances of the resource available. When the semaphore guards a single data structure, $N = 1$ means the semaphore is unlocked.

$N \leq 0$ No instances of the resource are available (or the semaphore is locked). $|N|$ is the number of processors waiting for the resource to become available.

The algorithm for acquiring (locking) such a semaphore is:

1. Decrement the semaphore value, N.

2. If N is less than 0, put my process ID in the $|N|$th slot of the queue of waiting processes, and wait for someone to tell me it's my turn.

The algorithm for releasing the semaphore is:

1. If N is less than 0, notify the process at the head of the queue that it's his turn, and adjust the queue accordingly.

2. Increment N.

Note that all accesses to the semaphore value and wait queue must be protected by spinlocks.

The **semop**() system call is a System V mechanism for implementing a more general version of counting/queuing semaphores. However, **semop**() does not guarantee that the first process in the queue will be the next to acquire the semaphore. For more information on **semop**(), refer to Chapter 6 and the **semop**(2) man page.

Spin or Block?

An important consideration that affects how you use semaphores is what a process should do while it is waiting. Four possibilities are:

- Don't wait. Do something else and check the semaphore later.

- Spin (busy wait). This minimizes overhead, but spinning for a long time (for example, during I/O operations) wastes processor cycles.

- Spin for a specified time (or number of loops), then block.

- Block (relinquish the processor to another job). Under certain circumstances, this may be the only acceptable course of action during potentially long waits. On the other hand, if your job needs to run at top priority with a minimum of overhead, you may choose to forego this courtesy at the expense of system throughput.

For example, a process that uses the **s_lock**() or **m_lock**() routine from the parallel-programming library spins until the requested lock is available. A process that uses the **semop**() system call blocks until the requested semaphore is available.

2.8.3 Events

An *event* is something that must happen before a task or process can proceed. Examples of events are:

- Completion of a task

- Appearance of a task in a formerly empty task queue

- Arrival of needed data

- Arrival of the last process at a synchronization point

Events have two values: posted and cleared. One or more processes *wait* for an event until another process *posts* the event. The waiting processes then proceed. The event may need to be *cleared* by the waiting process, by a master process, or by another process, depending on the program.

2.8.4 Barriers

A *barrier* is a synchronization point. The code executed at a barrier is usually something like this:

1. Mark myself (a process) as present at the barrier.

2. Wait for all the other processes to arrive.

3. Proceed.

The determination that all processes are present at the barrier may be made by the last process to arrive, by a master process, or by all processes independently.

2.8.5 Synchronization Costs

When you add locks and barriers to synchronize processes, you also add to execution time. If two or more processes try to access a locked variable at the same time, one process is granted the lock and the others spin until it is their turn. The processing time wasted is influenced by the number of times this occurs and the length of time each process holds the lock. Locks should be used only when necessary and held for as short a time as possible.

You can avoid contention for locks by creating a producer-consumer relationship between processes: only one process writes to a shared variable while the remaining processes read the variable. Refer to Appendix A for a sample C program that demonstrates a producer-consumer relationship between processes.

2.9 Input/Output

I/O in parallel programs is complicated by two factors:

- Use by parallel programs of standard I/O calls which create buffers in process-private memory—parallel processes are not synchronized when they read and write data.

- The tendency for a process to block (relinquish its processor) during an I/O operation.

These complications usually can be reduced by any of the following methods:

- Performing I/O only during sequential phases of the program

- Designating one process as a server to perform all I/O

- Allocating the standard I/O buffers in shared memory and using locks during buffered I/O operations

Implementing the third alternative is the most difficult because it must be done in a way that does not hamper the performance of sequential programs. Refer to Chapter 7 for more information on this topic.

2.10 Signals

Under DYNIX/ptx, you can use either the **sigset()** or **sigaction()** system call to manage signals. The functionality of these routines is equivalent, but the **sigaction()** system call supports a POSIX-compliant interface to signals. Both routines support reliable signals—once a handler is established for a particular signal, the specified action occurs for every occurrence of that signal until the default action is explicitly restored. However, you should use only one of these routines in a single application.

NOTE

*Use of the **signal()** system call is not recommended and may produce unexpected results.*

Also, the parallel-programming library uses the signal **SIGSEGV** *to grow stack and data space in shared memory. It also uses the signal* **SIGCHLD** *to terminate child processes correctly. Because of this, Sequent recommends that parallel programs do not include any special handling of either* **SIGSEGV** *or* **SIGCHLD** *signals.*

For more information on signals, refer to the **sigset(2)** and **sigaction(2)** man pages.

Chapter 3
Parallel-Programming Tools

Chapter 3
Parallel-Programming Tools

3.1 Introduction

This chapter describes some of the programming tools available on Symmetry systems. Some of these tools are available from Sequent and some have been developed by other vendors. Together, they show the range of parallel-programming approaches that are supported by Symmetry systems.

The applications that can be adapted for parallel programming vary greatly in their requirements for data sharing, interprocess communication, and synchronization. To gain optimal speedup from a parallel solution, the programmer must develop an algorithm that meets the requirements of the application while still exploiting all of its inherent parallelism. To aid in this effort, the programmer needs tools that adapt easily to the needs of a given application.

For example, a matrix multiplication on a large data set is best expressed in terms of data partitioning: the solution requires repeating the same operation on many different data items. This problem is very synchronous. The program has a well-defined beginning and end, and the programmer can easily predict at what points the processes must synchronize or communicate shared data. Ideal tools for this application would support creation and termination of multiple identical processes and division of shared data among processes.

In contrast, a large database application might be much better expressed in terms of function partitioning. At any time, different users may be using different utilities to access the database. These processes may need to communicate to share data, or one process may need to ensure that another process doesn't corrupt its data. This application is asynchronous: the programmer cannot predict when users will create processes that need to communicate or access shared data. This application requires tools that allow processes to communicate on an as-needed basis.

Symmetry systems support programming tools for a wide range of applications:

- The FORTRAN parallel-programming directives support parallel execution of FORTRAN DO loops. With these directives, you can execute many DO loops in parallel simply by adding a single line to the source code.

- The KAP/Sequent preprocessor identifies potential parallelism in FORTRAN programs and automatically restructures the programs for parallel execution.

- The microtasking routines in the parallel-programming library support data- and function-partitioning applications. They allow you to quickly and easily create sets of processes, schedule tasks among processes, and synchronize processes between tasks.

- The DYNIX/ptx operating system includes a number of facilities that support communication of data and status information between loosely related processes.

The following sections briefly describe these tools.

3.2 FORTRAN Parallel-Programming Directives

You can use the ptx/FORTRAN compiler to restructure DO loops for parallel execution in two ways:

- Manually, through insertion of parallel directives into your source code

- Automatically, using the KAP/Sequent preprocessor

If you choose the first method, you must insert directives that identify the loops to be executed in parallel, the shared and private data within each loop, and any critical sections of the loops (loop sections containing dependencies). You can also use these directives to control the scheduling of loop iterations among processes and the division of data among processes.

Once you have identified the parallel loops and properly marked the data and critical sections, the compiler handles all the low-level tasks of data partitioning. The compiler produces a program that transparently sets up shared data structures, creates a set of identical processes, schedules tasks among processes, and handles mutual exclusion and process synchronization.

Chapter 4 explains how to use the FORTRAN parallel-programming directives and how to analyze DO loops to identify shared and private data and critical code sections.

To insert parallel FORTRAN directives automatically into your FORTRAN source code, use the KAP/Sequent preprocessor.

3.2.1 KAP/Sequent Preprocessor

The KAP/Sequent preprocessor is an optimizing preprocessor that identifies potential parallelism within FORTRAN code and restructures the code for parallel execution on a Symmetry system. This optional product is only available from Kuck and Associates, Inc.

You can invoke KAP/Sequent with the **–K** compile-time option or as a standalone preprocessor. KAP/Sequent requires no programmer intervention, although you can add directives or provide additional information to direct the preprocessor to do further restructuring.

KAP/Sequent performs the following code optimizations:

- Concurrentization
- Synchronization
- Local variable identification
- Recognition of sum, dot-product, and MAX and MIN reductions
- Recognition of parallel-programming library calls
- Loop reordering
- Induction variable recognition
- Global forward substitution
- Variable lifetime analysis
- Loop peeling
- Some "dusty-deck" transformations

The KAP/Sequent listing displays the restructured program along with the following information:

- Annotated listing of the restructured program
- Summary of optimizations performed
- Compilation performance statistics
- Original source line number next to each line of the optimized program
- Graphical marking of DO loops
- Footnotes describing details of optimizations
- Embedded syntax error and warning messages

For example, consider the following sequential program in the source file *matmul.f*:

```
        SUBROUTINE MATMUL(N,R,S,T)
C
C Perform a matrix multiply for N by N matrices R and S
C and store the result in matrix T
C
        INTEGER*4 I, J, K, N
        REAL*4 R(N,N), S(N,N), T(N,N)
C
        DO 10 J = 1, N
        DO 10 I = 1, N
        DO 10 K = 1, N
           T(I,J) = T(I,J) + R(I,K) * S(K,J)
   10   CONTINUE
        RETURN
        END
```

Entering the following command runs the KAP/Sequent preprocessor, and compiles and links the program to produce the object file *matmul.o*.

fortran –K –c matmul.f

Running the KAP/Sequent preprocessor also produces the output file *matmul.cmp*, which contains a listing of the transformed source file:

```
C       KAP/SEQUENT   7.3 k070111 890428 o3,r3,d3 date time
        SUBROUTINE MATMUL(N,R,S,T)
C
C Perform a matrix multiply for N by N matrices R and S
C and store the result in matrix T
C
        INTEGER*4 I, J, K, N
        REAL*4 R(N,N), S(N,N), T(N,N)
C
C$DOACROSS SHARE(N,T,R,S),LASTLOCAL(K,I)
        DO 10 J=1,N
        DO 10 K=1,N
        DO 2 I=1,N
           T(I,J) = T(I,J) + R(I,K) * S(K,J)
      2 CONTINUE
   10   CONTINUE
        RETURN
        END
```

Notice that the KAP/Sequent preprocessor automatically included the FORTRAN parallel-programming directive C$DOACROSS. The preprocessor also optimized the code by changing the order of the DO loops so that the outermost loop became the innermost loop. By doing this, there is no communication between iterations of the inner loop. (Refer to Chapter 4 for information on the FORTRAN parallel-programming directives.)

For more information on KAP/Sequent, refer to the *KAP/Sequent User's Guide*.

3.3 The Parallel-Programming Library

The Sequent parallel-programming library is a set of C routines and macros that allow you to execute C, C++, FORTRAN, or Pascal subprograms in parallel. The library includes routines to handle the following functions:

- Allocation of memory for shared data
- Creation of processes to execute subprograms in parallel
- Identification of individual processes
- Suspension of processes during serial program sections
- Mutual exclusion on shared data
- Synchronization of processes during critical sections

Programs that use the parallel-programming library can be made to automatically balance loads between processors and to automatically adjust the division of computing tasks at run time based on the number of processors configured in the system. The library routines allow you to handle the communication and synchronization needs of an algorithm at a high level while concentrating on the design of the parallel algorithm. Table 3-1 lists and briefly describes the routines in the parallel-programming library.

Table 3-1
Parallel-Programming Library Routines

Routine	Description
cpus_online	Return number of CPUs online
m_fork, p_fork	Execute a subprogram in parallel. (p_fork is used for PASCAL programs only.)
m_get_myid	Return process identification number.
m_get_numprocs	Return number of child processes.
m_kill_procs	Terminate child processes.

Table 3-1
Parallel-Programming Library Routines (cont.)

Routine	Description
m_lock	Lock a lock.
m_multi	End single-process code section.
m_next	Increment global counter.
m_park_procs	Suspend child process execution.
m_rele_procs	Resume child process execution.
m_set_procs	Set number of child processes.
m_single	Begin single-process code section.
m_sync	Check in at barrier.
m_unlock	Unlock a lock.
s_init_barrier	Initialize a barrier.
S_INIT_BARRIER	C macro version of s_init_barrier.
s_init_lock	Initialize a lock.
S_INIT_LOCK	C macro version of s_init_lock.
s_lock or s_clock	Lock a lock.
S_LOCK or S_CLOCK	C macro versions of s_lock and s_clock, respectively.
s_unlock	Unlock a lock.
S_UNLOCK	C macro version of s_unlock.
s_wait_barrier	Wait at a barrier.
S_WAIT_BARRIER	C macro version of s_wait_barrier.

Table 3-1
Parallel-Programming Library Routines (cont.)

Routine	Description
sbrk or brk	Change private data segment size.
shbrk or shsbrk	Change shared data segment size.
shfree	Deallocate shared data memory.
shmalloc or shrealloc	Allocate shared data memory.

As you can see, there are three distinct groups of routines: routines beginning with the characters "m_", routines beginning with the characters "s_" or "S_", and routines beginning with the characters "sh". These are the microtasking routines, the multitasking routines, and the shared-memory management routines, respectively. These routines are described in detailed in
Appendix B. Chapters 5 and 6 describe how to use these routines in both data- and function-partitioning applications.

3.4 Other Tools

Most applications that are coded for sequential execution can be easily recoded for parallel execution. The programming tools described in this chapter can be applied to a wide range of applications, and parallel programmers are constantly developing new tools that can be run on Sequent systems. With its symmetric architecture, shared memory, and built-in parallel-programming support, the Sequent architecture can support almost any application and parallel-programming model. Since new tools are being developed daily, you should consult your Marketing representative about current information on available parallel-programming tools.

Tables

Chapter 4
Data Partitioning with ptx/FORTRAN

4.1 Introduction

This chapter explains how to convert FORTRAN DO loops for data partitioning. The ptx/FORTRAN compiler recognizes a set of special directives for parallel loops. With these directives, you mark the loop to be executed in parallel and classify loop variables so that data is passed correctly between loop iterations. The ptx/FORTRAN compiler interprets the directives and restructures the source code for data partitioning. In addition, the compiler inserts calls to the parallel-programming library and directs the linker to place variables in the appropriate area of memory.

4.2 Selecting a Loop for Parallel Execution

There are three criteria you should use when selecting a loop for parallel execution:

- If possible, choose the outermost loop in a program or program section.

- Always choose a loop that accounts for a large portion of the computation done by the program.

- Whenever possible, choose an independent loop.

You can use the **prof** utility to determine which loops are responsible for the most computation. Refer to Chapter 7 for more information about **prof**.

Ideally, the loops you choose for parallel execution should be *independent loops*, loops in which no iteration depends on the operations in any other iteration. You can determine whether a loop is independent by answering the following question:

> *If this loop were executed one iteration at a time but in random order, would it still produce correct results?*

If the answer is yes, the loop is independent; if not, then the loop is dependent. If you determine that a loop is dependent, but the dependencies account for only a small portion of the processing done by the loop, there is still an advantage to executing the loop in parallel. You may even be able to minimize the impact of these dependencies on execution time by moving the statements that carry dependencies closer together.

4.3 Preparing DO Loops

To prepare a DO loop for parallel execution, follow these steps:

1. Analyze the variables in the loop and classify them according to usage. (Section 4.3.1 explains how to analyze variable usage.)

2. Use the parallel-programming directives to identify the loop to be executed in parallel and to specify the class for each variable in the loop. (Section 4.3.2 explains how to use the parallel programming directives.)

3. Use the parallel-programming directives or the parallel-programming library routines to preserve correct data and control flow within the loop. (Refer to Section 4.3.2 for additional information on when and how to perform this step).

4.3.1 Analyzing Variable Usage

The first step in preparing a FORTRAN DO loop for data partitioning is to analyze how each variable in the loop is used. You have already done some of this when you determined which loop to execute in parallel—you analyzed variable usage to determine which loops were independent. Now you need to examine each variable in the loop and classify it as belonging to one of the following categories:

- Shared variables

- Local variables

- Reduction variables

- Shared ordered variables

- Shared locked variables

NOTE

The loop index is not considered to be a variable within the loop. There is no need to analyze its usage unless it is referenced elsewhere in the DO loop. If the loop index is referenced in the body of the loop and you do not explicitly classify it, the compiler automatically classifies the variable as LASTLOCAL *(described on the following page).*

Other variables appearing in the loop control statement do not need to be analyzed unless they also appear within the body of the loop.

The remainder of this chapter explains how to identify each kind of variable and presents a worksheet to aid you in classifying the variables in your program. The code segments presented in this chapter are used to illustrate different variable classifications and should not be viewed as complete programs. For a complete listing of a parallel application coded in FORTRAN, refer to Appendix A.

Shared Variables

A shared variable is an array or scalar (single-element) variable that has *one* of the following properties:

- It is *read-only*; that is, it is read but never written within the loop.

- It is an array in which each element is referenced by only one loop iteration. (This can occur when the array index varies directly with the loop index.)

In the following example loop, all the variables except k, the DO-loop index, are shared:

```
        DO 1 k = 1,n
   1        X(k) = Q + Y(k)*(R*Z(k+10) + T*Z(k+11))
```

The variables Q, Y, R, Z, and T meet the first test for a shared variable: they are never assigned values within the loop. The only variable that appears on the left side of an assignment statement is X, which meets the second test for a shared variable: it is an array and each element is read and written by only one iteration. (You can tell because its index varies directly with the loop index.)

Local Variables

A local variable is a variable that is initialized in each loop iteration before its value is used. The compiler recognizes two types of local variables: LOCAL and LASTLOCAL. A variable is classified as LOCAL if it is not used to pass data values in or out of the loop or between loop iterations. A variable is classified as LASTLOCAL if the value assigned to the variable in the last loop iteration is available after the loop is exited. By default, the DO-loop index is a LASTLOCAL variable.

The following example loop contains both shared and local variables. Note that the variable i should be classified since it is used in the body of the loop. Also, assume that the outermost loop is the one to be executed in parallel.

```
      DO 10 i = 1,n
      DO 10 k = 1,n
      DO 10 j = 1,n
        R(i,j) = R(i,j) + S(i,k) * T(k,j)
 10     CONTINUE
```

In this loop, the variables R, S, T, and n are all shared: S, T, and n are all read-only, and R is an array whose index varies directly with the loop index. The variables i, j, and k are local: they are not read-only and they are initialized by each iteration before they are used in any operation.

Reduction Variables

A reduction variable is an array or scalar variable that has the following properties:

- It is used in only one associative, commutative operation within the loop. (These operations include addition or subtraction, multiplication or division, logical AND, logical OR, exclusive OR, MIN, and MAX.)

- The operation must be of the following form:

  var = var op expr

  var is the reduction variable, *op* is an associative, commutative operation, and *expr* is an expression that does not include the variable *var*. The variable may occur in more than one such statement, as long as the operation is the same.

NOTE

For reduction variables, subtraction and division are treated as addition and multiplication of inverses.

The MIN and MAX intrinsic functions are recognized as providing the correct form for a reduction operation. For more information on these functions, refer to the ptx/FORTRAN User's Manual.

The following example loop contains a reduction variable:

```
          DO 66666 k = 1,i-1
              Q = Q + B(i,k) * W(i-k)
  66666    CONTINUE
```

In this loop, the variables B, W, and i are shared, because they are read-only within the loop. The variable Q is a reduction variable. It is used in a single associative, commutative operation (addition) and the operation has the correct form.

Shared Ordered Variables

A shared ordered variable is an array or scalar variable that has the following properties:

- It does not qualify as a shared, local, or reduction variable.

- If the loop iterations were executed (to completion) one at a time in random order, the operations involving the variable would not produce correct results.

The following example loop contains two shared ordered variables. Assume that dx and dy are not referenced outside of the loop.

```
      do 10 i = 1, n-1
         x(i) = xa(i) + xb(i)
         dx = x(i) - x(i+1)
         y(i) = ya(i) + yb(i)
         dy = y(i) - y(i+1)
         rho(i) = sqrt(dx * dx + dy * dy)
   10 continue
```

In this loop, the variables xa, xb, ya, and yb are shared: they are all read-only. The variables dx and dy are local: they are initialized in each loop iteration before their values are used and they are not referenced outside the loop. The variables x and y are shared ordered since executing the loop iterations in random order would produce different values than when the loop is executed in sequential order.

Shared Locked Variables

Shared locked variables include all the variables that do not fit into any of the other categories. A shared locked variable is an array or scalar variable that has the following properties:

- It can be read and written by more than one loop iteration.

- If the loop iterations were executed (to completion) one at a time in random order, the operations involving the variable would not produce correct results.

The first of these characteristics makes the difference between a simple shared variable and a shared locked variable. Because a shared locked variable can be read and written by more than one loop iteration and because loop iterations will execute simultaneously, you must ensure that only one loop iteration is using the variable at a time. The mechanism to do this is a lock, hence the name *shared locked variable*.

The following example computes the distance between one city and a number of other cities, then compares each distance with the minimum distance and selects the array index of the nearest city. This loop contains two shared locked variables:

```
      x = 1
      y = 2
      least = 9999999.0
      DO 10 i = 1,n
          xsqdis = (BVRTN(x)-A(i,x))**2
          ysqdis = (BVRTN(y)-A(i,y))**2
          dist = SQRT(xsqdis + ysqdis)
          IF (dist.LT.least) THEN
              closest = i
              least = dist
          ENDIF
 10   CONTINUE
```

In this loop, the variables BVRTN and A are shared: they are read-only within the loop. The variables xsqdis, ysqdis, and dist are local: they are written in each iteration before they are read. The variables closest and least are shared locked: they are read and written by each loop iteration, but the order in which the iterations are executed does not affect the results of the operations involving them. As long as the loop is executed n times, dist will be compared with each value of least. As long as nothing changes the value of closest or least between the IF statement and either assignment statement, the loop will return the correct answers.

Variable-Analysis Worksheet

As you analyze the variables in your loop, you may find it helpful to use the worksheet shown in Figure 4-1.

	SHARED	LOCAL	LASTLOCAL	REDUCTION	SHARED ORDERED	SHARED LOCKED
VARIABLE NAME	*Is the variable read-only within the loop OR is it an array where each element is read and written by only one loop iteration?*	*Could the variable be renamed in each iteration without affecting the program result AND can the value be undefined after exiting the loop?*	*Could the variable be renamed in each iteration without affecting the program result AND should the value be defined after exiting the loop?*	*Is the variable used in only one associative, commutative operation within the loop AND is it always read, then written?*	*If the loop iterations were executed in random order, would the operations involving this variable produce different results?*	*Have you answered "no" to all the other questions?*

Figure 4-1. Variable-analysis worksheet.

To use this worksheet, simply list all the variables in your loop in the first column. For each variable, mark in the answers to the listed questions until you answer "yes" to a question. When you mark a "yes" in any column, you'll find the variable type in the label at the top of the column. Section 4.3.2 shows some completed worksheets.

4.3.2 Preparing the loop

Once you have analyzed the variables in your loop, you are ready to use the FORTRAN parallel-programming directives to prepare the loop for parallel execution. Table 4-1 lists the parallel-programming directives.

Table 4-1
FORTRAN Parallel-Programming Directives

Directive	Description
C$	Add FORTRAN statement for conditional compilation.
C$DOACROSS	Identify DO loop for parallel execution.
C$LOCK and C$UNLOCK	Identify a parallel do loop section which must be executed by one process at a time.
C$ORDER and C$ENDORDER	Identify a parallel do loop section which contains a shared ordered variable.
C$&	Continue parallel-programming directive.

If your loop has any shared locked variables, you can use the parallel-programming library routines **m_lock()** and **m_unlock()** or the C$LOCK and C$UNLOCK directives to mark the loop sections containing the shared locked variables. Refer to the "Marking Locked Sections" section later in this chapter for more information on this topic.

Marking the Parallel Loop

The first step in preparing the loop for parallel execution is to add a C$DOACROSS directive on the line *immediately* preceding the DO statement. The C$DOACROSS directive looks like this:

```
C$DOACROSS  option [ , option . . . ]
```

option can be one or more of the options listed in Table 4-2.

Table 4-2
C$DOACROSS options

Option	Description
SHARE	Specifies variable is shared among all processes.
LOCAL	Specifies variable is local to each process.
LASTLOCAL	Specifies local variable whose value must be available after exit from a loop.
LOCKS	Identifies a DO loop section which must be executed by one process at a time.
REDUCTIONS	Specifies a reduction variable within a loop.
ORDER	Identifies a code section which must be executed serially in loop iteration order.
CHUNK	specifies how many loop iterations each process should execute before participating in a dynamic rescheduling. (The compiler treats this value as a suggestion only.)

These options fall into two categories: the SHARE, LOCAL, LASTLOCAL, LOCKS, REDUCTION and ORDER options are used to control data flow between parallel loop iterations, while the CHUNK option is used to minimize dynamic scheduling overhead. For more information on these options refer to the *ptx/FORTRAN User's Manual*.

To mark a loop with the C$DOACROSS directive, follow this procedure:

1. Insert a C$DOACROSS directive on a line *immediately* before the DO statement.

2. Add the SHARE option to the C$DOACROSS statement and list in parentheses all the shared, shared ordered, and shared locked variables from your worksheet.

3. If your loop includes any local variables, do the following:

   • If the value assigned to the variable in the last loop iteration must be available after exiting the loop, add the LASTLOCAL option and list these variables in parentheses.

   • If the value can be undefined after exiting the loop, add the LOCAL option and list these variables in parentheses.

4. If your loop includes any reduction variables, add the REDUCTION option and list in parentheses all the reduction variables from the worksheet.

5. If the loop contains any shared ordered variables, add the ORDER option, choose names for the loop sections containing the variables, and list the names in parentheses. You can use any valid fortran name for an ordered section.

6. If you have a loop with a large number of iterations and you are using dynamic scheduling, you may want to use the CHUNK option.

7. Finally, if the loop contains any shared locked variables, mark the loop with the LOCKS option.

If the C$DOACROSS directive is too long, you can use the C$& directive to continue it onto a new line.

Let's look at an example loop from section 4.3.1 and see how to mark it with a C$DOACROSS directive. The following example, a matrix product, has four shared variables and three local variables. Assume for this example that the values of i, j, and k are not referenced outside the body of the loop.

```
        DO 10 i = 1,n
        DO 10 k = 1,n
        DO 10 j = 1,n
          R(i,j) = R(i,j) + S(i,k) * T(k,j)
   10   CONTINUE
```

Figure 4-2 shows the completed variable analysis worksheet for this loop.

VARIABLE NAME	SHARED *Is the variable read-only within the loop OR is it an array where each element is read and written by only one loop iteration?*	LOCAL *Could the variable be renamed in each iteration without affecting the program result AND can the value be undefined after exiting the loop?*	LASTLOCAL *Could the variable be renamed in each iteration without affecting the program result AND should the value be defined after exiting the loop?*	REDUCTION *Is the variable used in only one associative, commutative operation within the loop AND is it always read, then written?*	SHARED ORDERED *If the loop iterations were executed in random order, would the operations involving this variable produce different results?*	SHARED LOCKED *Have you answered "no" to all the other questions?*
i	no	yes				
k	no	yes				
j	no	yes				
n	yes					
R	yes					
S	yes					
T	yes					

Figure 4-2. Variable-analysis worksheet for independent loop.

When the C$DOACROSS statement is added, using the information from the worksheet, the loop looks like this:

```
C$DOACROSS SHARE(R, S, T, n), LOCAL(i, k, j)
        DO 10 i = 1,n
        DO 10 k = 1,n
        DO 10 j = 1,n
          R(i,j) = R(i,j) + S(i,k) * T(k,j)
    10    CONTINUE
```

NOTE

The C$DOACROSS *directive must start in column 1, just like a FORTRAN comment line. If you run the FORTRAN compiler without the parallel option (–mp), the compiler treats these directives as comment statements.*

Marking Ordered Sections

The C$ORDER and C$ENDORDER directives mark the beginning and end of a loop section containing a shared ordered variable. The C$ORDER directive appears on the line immediately preceding the first reference to the variable, and the C$ENDORDER directive appears on the line immediately following the last reference to the variable. (Actually, there are more exact rules for placing these directives for highly optimized execution, but such placement requires more complex evaluation of the order dependency. Refer to the section labeled "Optimizing Ordered Sections" later in this chapter for a discussion of this evaluation.)

These directives look like this:

```
        C$ORDER section_name
        C$ENDORDER section_name
```

The *section_name* parameter can be any valid FORTRAN name. The section name in the C$ENDORDER directive must match the name in the corresponding C$ORDER directive, and both must match a name declared with the C$DOACROSS ORDER option. The section name cannot be used for any other purpose within the program.

NOTE

You must ensure that each C$ORDER/C$ENDORDER pair is executed exactly once by each loop iteration. Each loop iteration waits at a C$ORDER directive for the previous iteration to execute the corresponding C$ENDORDER directive before executing the ordered section. If an iteration fails to execute an ordered section (for example, because of a conditional branch), the subsequent iterations can never execute that ordered section, and the program hangs. If a parallel loop contains a conditional branch, you can place a pair of identical C$ORDER/C$ENDORDER directives within each branch. The duplicate pair can enclose an empty section.

Now let's complete the example ordered loop from section 4.3.1. This example has four shared variables, two local variables, and two shared ordered variables.

```
      do 10 i = 1, n-1
        x(i) = xa(i) + xb(i)
        dx = x(i) - x(i+1)
        y(i) = ya(i) + yb(i)
        dy = y(i) - y(i+1)
        rho(i) = sqrt(dx * dx + dy * dy)
  10  continue
```

Figure 4-3 shows the completed variable-analysis worksheet for this loop.

VARIABLE NAME	SHARED *Is the variable read-only within the loop OR is it an array where each element is read and written by only one loop iteration?*	LOCAL *Could the variable be renamed in each iteration without affecting the program result AND can the value be undefined after exiting the loop?*	LASTLOCAL *Could the variable be renamed in each iteration without affecting the program result AND should the value be defined after exiting the loop?*	REDUCTION *Is the variable used in only one associative, commutative operation within the loop AND is it always read, then written?*	SHARED ORDERED *If the loop iterations were executed in random order, would the operations involving this variable produce different results?*	SHARED LOCKED *Have you answered "no" to all the other questions?*
xa	yes					
xb	yes					
ya	yes					
yb	yes					
x	no	no	no	no	yes	
y	no	no	no	no	yes	
dx	no	yes				
dy	no	yes				

Figure 4-3. Variable-analysis worksheet for ordered loop.

Once the C$DOACROSS directive is added using the information from the worksheet, the loop looks like the following (assume dx and dy are not referenced outside the body of the loop).

```
c$doacross order(gx,gy),share(x,xa,xb,y,ya,yb,rho),
c$& local(dx,dy)
    do 10 i = 1, n-1
c$order gx
      x(i) = xa(i) + xb(i)
      dx = x(i) - x(i+1)
c$endorder gx
c$order gy
      y(i) = ya(i) + yb(i)
      dy = y(i) - y(i+1)
c$endorder gy
      rho(i) = sqrt(dx * dx + dy * dy)
10  continue
```

In this example, the programmer has chosen the names gx and gy for the
code sections containing the variables x and y and included the C$ORDER
and C$ENDORDER directives to mark these sections. Also, notice the use of
the C$& directive to continue the C$DOACROSS directive to a new line.

Marking Locked Sections

To mark the beginning and end of a loop section containing a shared locked
variable, you can do one of the following:

- Use the C$LOCK and C$UNLOCK directives in conjunction with the
  C$DOACROSS LOCKS option

- Use the parallel-programming library routines **m_lock**() and
  m_unlock()

Sequent recommends the use of the C$LOCK and C$UNLOCK directives over
the **m_lock**() and **m_unlock**() routines.

Now let's complete the example ordered loop from section 4.3.1. This example has two shared locked variables. (Assume that the variable closest has been declared as an integer.)

```
        x = 1
        y = 2
        least = 9999999.0
        DO 10 i = 1,n
            xsqdis = (BVRTN(x)-A(i,x))**2
            ysqdis = (BVRTN(y)-A(i,y))**2
            dist = SQRT(xsqdis + ysqdis)
            IF (dist.LT.least) THEN
                closest = i
                least = dist
            ENDIF
 10     CONTINUE
```

Figure 4-4 shows the completed variable-analysis worksheet for this loop.

VARIABLE NAME	SHARED	LOCAL	LASTLOCAL	REDUCTION	SHARED ORDERED	SHARED LOCKED
	Is the variable read-only within the loop OR is it an array where each element is read and written by only one loop iteration?	*Could the variable be renamed in each iteration without affecting the program result AND can the value be undefined after exiting the loop?*	*Could the variable be renamed in each iteration without affecting the program result AND should the value be defined after exiting the loop?*	*Is the variable used in only one associative, commutative operation within the loop AND is it always read, then written?*	*If the loop iterations were executed in random order, would the operations involving this variable produce different results?*	*Have you answered "no" to all the other questions?*
BVRTN	yes					
A	yes					
xsqdis	no	yes				
ysqdis	no	yes				
dist	no	yes				
closest	no	no	no	no	no	yes
least	no	no	no	no	no	yes
x	yes					
y	yes					

Figure 4-4.   Variable-analysis worksheet for shared locked loop.

When the C$DOACROSS statement is added, using the information from the worksheet, the loop looks like this:

```
          x = 1
          y = 2
          least = 9999999.0
C$DOACROSS SHARE(BVRTN,A,closest,least,x,y),
C$&              LOCAL(xsqdis,ysqdis,dist)
          DO 10 i = 1,n
             xsqdis = (BVRTN(x)-A(i,x))**2
             ysqdis = (BVRTN(y)-A(i,y))**2
             dist = SQRT(xsqdis + ysqdis)
             IF (dist.LT.least) THEN
                closest = i
                least = dist
             ENDIF
      10  CONTINUE
```

To complete the preparation of this loop, you must add the C$LOCK and C$UNLOCK directives to protect the section containing closest and least. With these directives added, the loop looks like this:

```
          x = 1
          y = 2
          least = 9999999.0
C$DOACROSS SHARE(BVRTN,A,closest,least,x,y),
C$&              LOCAL(xsqdis,ysqdis,dist), LOCKS(iguard)
          DO 10 i = 1,n
             xsqdis = (BVRTN(x)-A(i,x))**2
             ysqdis = (BVRTN(y)-A(i,y))**2
             dist = SQRT(xsqdis + ysqdis)
C$LOCK iguard
             IF (dist.LT.least) THEN
                closest = i
                least = dist
             ENDIF
C$UNLOCK iguard
      10  CONTINUE
```

You could use the **m_lock**() and **m_unlock**() routines instead of the C$LOCK and C$UNLOCK directives. The call to **m_lock**() should appear on the line immediately preceding the first reference to the variable, and the call to **m_unlock**() should appear on the line following the last reference to the variable.

Calls to these routines look like this:

```
CALL m_lock
CALL m_unlock
```

You may want the **m_lock**() and **m_unlock**() calls compiled only when the parallel option is specified. To do this, begin the call statements with the C$ directive. (This directive allows you to insert any valid FORTRAN statement into a program and have it compiled only when the **–mp** option is specified.)

Using **m_lock**() and **m_unlock**(), the loop now looks like this:

```
        x = 1
        y = 2
        least = 9999999.0
C$DOACROSS SHARE (BVRTN, A,closest,least,x,y),
C$&            LOCAL(xsqdis,ysqdis,dist)
        DO 10 i = 1,n
            xsqdis = (BVRTN(x)-A(i,x))**2
            ysqdis = (BVRTN(y)-A(i,y))**2
            dist = SQRT(xsqdis + ysqdis)
C$          CALL m_lock
            IF (dist.LT.least) THEN
                closest = i
                least = dist
            ENDIF
C$          CALL m_unlock
    10    CONTINUE
```

The **m_lock**() and **m_unlock**() routines ensure that only one loop iteration can execute the locked section at a time.

Optimizing Ordered Sections

When executing loops in parallel, the goal is to minimize the amount of code in synchronized sections. In the case of FORTRAN DO loops, this means placing the `C$ORDER` and `C$ENDORDER` directives as close together as possible. The following simple rule allows you to minimize ordered DO loop sections: for any two statements, x and y, such that y must be executed after the x statement in a previous loop iteration, the `C$ORDER` and `C$ENDORDER` statements must be placed as follows:

- The `C$ORDER` directive must precede statement y.

- The `C$ENDORDER` directive must follow statement x.

- The `C$ORDER` directive must precede the `C$ENDORDER` directive.

To illustrate how this rule is applied, let's examine the following example loop:

```
      DO 10 i = 2,n
   20    a(i) = c(i) * pi          ! statement x
   30    b(i) = a(i-1) * d(i)      ! statement y
   10 CONTINUE
```

In each iteration of this loop, the value of `b(i)` depends on the value of `a(i)` produced in the previous iteration. Applying the rule stated above, the `C$ORDER` statement must precede statement 30, the `C$ENDORDER` statement must follow statement 20, and the `C$ORDER` statement must precede the `C$ENDORDER` statement. When the directives are inserted according to these rules, the loop looks like this:

```
   C$DOACROSS SHARE(a, b, c, d, pi), ORDER(iguard)
      DO 10 i = 2,n
   20    a(i) = c(i) * pi          ! statement x
   C$ORDER iguard
   C$ENDORDER iguard
   30    b(i) = a(i-1) * d(i)      ! statement y
   10 CONTINUE
```

The ordered section is now very short. In fact, it now encloses no program statements. The C$ORDER directive halts execution of statement 30 of this loop iteration until the C$ENDORDER in the previous iteration is executed. The C$ENDORDER is a signal that statement 20 has been executed and execution of statement 30 can begin for the next loop iteration.

There are two further easy optimizations for ordered sections. First, if an ordered section is nested within another, the inner ordered section requires no C$ORDER and C$ENDORDER statements. Second, if all the ordered sections in a loop are empty (as in the previous example), then there may be some benefit in splitting the loop into several loops at the ordered sections and placing the loops in order. This loop splitting transforms the single loop into a series of loops with no synchronization. (Remember, only one DO loop executes at a time.) This method is efficient only when the number of processors is very large and the code within the loop is very small. You will have to determine whether the additional loop overhead outweighs the benefits of eliminating ordered sections. You can use the microsecond clock and execute the program both ways to determine which method provides the best results. The following example illustrates the use of this technique:

```
      DO 10 i = 2,n
         a(i) = c(i) * pi
   10 CONTINUE
      DO 20 i = 2,n
         b(i) = a(i-1) * d(i)
   20 CONTINUE
```

4.4 Compiling, Executing, and Debugging

To complete development of your data-partitioned FORTRAN program, follow this procedure:

1. Invoke the ptx/FORTRAN compiler with the **–mp** option. This directs the compiler to convert each parallel DO loop into a subroutine and add code to dynamically assign copies of the subroutine to different processes for execution.

2. Execute the program and check the results.

3. If necessary, use the parallel symbolic debugger, invoked with the **pdbx** command, to debug the program.

4.4.1 Compiling a FORTRAN Program

To compile and link a program, enter the following command:

fortran –mp *sourcefile.f*

When this command is executed, the compiler links in the parallel-programming library and produces an executable file named *a.out*.

If you link the program separately from the compile step using the **ld** command, you need to include the **–lpps** and **–lseq** options on the **ld** command line. If you compile program units separately, be sure to specify the **–mp** option for each compilation to ensure that all common variables are placed in shared memory.

For more information on parallel-programming directives or the FORTRAN compiler and its options, refer to the *ptx/FORTRAN User's Manual*. For more information on the DYNIX/ptx linker, refer to the **ld**(1) man page.

4.4.2 Executing the Program

To execute the program, simply enter the name of the executable file from your shell. The default name of the executable file is *a.out*.

4.4.3 Debugging the Program

If your program produces incorrect results, you can use the DYNIX/ptx debugger, Pdbx, to isolate any problems. Pdbx is a symbolic debugger based on **dbx**, a debugger widely used in UNIX systems. Use the **pdbx** command to invoke the debugger when debugging parallel programs; otherwise, use the **dbx** command.

When debugging programs that use the parallel-programming library, remember that by default the debugger takes a breakpoint upon exiting from child processes. When the debugger encounters these breakpoints, you must enter (Ctrl-Z) to return control to the debugger and continue execution. To disable the automatic breakpoint, use the debugger command **ignore exit**.

The parallel-programming library uses the signal **SIGSEGV** to determine when to allocate more space for a process's shared stack. The debugger automatically stops whenever this signal is encountered. To disable these automatic breakpoints, use the command **ignore sigsegv**. For more information on the debugger, refer to the *Pdbx User's Manual*.

For more information on Pdbx, refer to the *Pdbx User's Manual*.

Chapter 5
Data Partitioning with DYNIX/ptx

Figures

Tables

Chapter 5
Data Partitioning with DYNIX/ptx

5.1 Introduction

This chapter explains how to structure C, C++, Pascal, and FORTRAN programs for data partitioning, and how to use the DYNIX/ptx parallel-programming library to execute loops in parallel.

The ptx/FORTRAN compiler recognizes special directives for data partitioning of DO loops. If you want to data partition a FORTRAN DO loop, refer to Chapter 4.

NOTE

The examples in this chapter are written in C, but the discussion and instructions apply to FORTRAN, C, C++, and Pascal programs.

5.2 The Microtasking Method

The data-partitioning method described in this chapter is sometimes called microtasking. As you may recall from Chapter 2, microtasking programs create multiple independent processes to execute loop iterations in parallel. The microtasking method has the following characteristics:

- The parallel processes share some data and create their own private copies of other data.

- The division of the computing load adjusts automatically to the number of available processes.

- The program controls data flow and synchronization by using tools specially designed for data partitioning.

You determine which data is shared between parallel processes and how the program adjusts to the number of available CPUs. (Sections 5.4 and 5.5 explain how to do this.) The parallel-programming library contains the tools to create and control parallel processes in your microtasking program and is described in section 5.3.

A microtasking program works like this:

- Each loop to be executed in parallel is contained in a subprogram.

- For each loop, the program calls a special function which forks a set of child processes and assigns an identical copy of the subprogram to each process for parallel execution. The special function creates a copy of any private data for each process.

- Each copy of the subprogram executes some of the loop iterations. You can set up the subprogram to use either static scheduling or dynamic scheduling.

- If the loop being executed in parallel is not completely independent, the subprogram may contain calls to functions that synchronize the parallel processes at critical points by using locks, barriers, and other semaphores.

- When all the loop iterations have been executed, control returns from the subprogram. At this point, the program either terminates the parallel processes, suspends their execution until they are needed to execute another subprogram, or leaves them to spin until they are needed again.

5.3 The Parallel-Programming Library

The parallel-programming library includes three sets of routines: a microtasking library, a multitasking library, and a set of routines for shared memory allocation. Sections 5.3.1 through 5.3.3 describe these sets of routines and Appendix B lists the man pages for each routine.

NOTE

The parallel-programming library is compatible with ptx/PASCAL (invoked as **pce** *or* **pascal***), not with Berkeley Pascal.*

When you store a program variable in shared memory and the process containing that variable is swapped out of memory, the parallel-programming library may temporarily store the information in shared memory in one or more disk files. Depending on the availability of file space on your system, you may wish to specify where these temporary files are created with the **TMPPATH** environment variable. The parallel-programming library attempts to open these files in the following areas in the indicated order:

1. The directory specified by the environment variable **TMPPATH**

2. The current working directory, "."

3. The directory specified by the environment variable **HOME**

4. */usr/tmp*

5. */tmp*

If you kill a parallel program during shared-memory initialization, you may have to delete these temporary files manually using the **rm** command. These files are named *shared data process_id* and *stack data process_id*, where process_id is the process identification (both filenames contain several blank characters). Generally, manual removal of these files is unnecessary and the existence of these files will be invisible.

5.3.1 The Microtasking Routines

Using the microtasking routines, you can fork a set of child processes, assign the processes to execute loop iterations in parallel, and synchronize the processes as necessary to provide proper data flow between loop iterations. Table 5-1 lists the microtasking routines in the parallel-programming library.

Table 5-1
Parallel-Programming Library Microtasking Routines

Routine	Description
m_fork, p_fork	Execute a subprogram in parallel. (p_fork is used for PASCAL programs only.)
m_get_myid	Return process identification number.
m_get_numprocs	Return number of child processes.
m_kill_procs	Terminate child processes.
m_lock	Lock a lock.
m_next	Increment global counter.
m_park_procs	Suspend child process execution.
m_rele_procs	Resume child process execution.
m_set_procs	Set number of child processes.
m_sync	Check in at barrier.
m_unlock	Unlock a lock.

NOTE

The microtasking library is designed around the routines **m_fork** *or* **p_fork** *(Use* **p_fork** *in Pascal programs only). Other microtasking routines should be used only in combination with one of these routines. Otherwise, they can cause unexpected side effects.*

5.3.2 Multitasking Routines

The general-purpose multitasking routines include a routine to determine the number of available CPUs and several process synchronization routines that are more flexible than those available in the microtasking library. Table 5-2 lists the general-purpose multitasking routines in the parallel-programming library.

Table 5-2
Parallel-Programming Library Multitasking Routines

Routine	Description
cpus_online	Return number of CPUs online.
s_init_barrier	Initialize a barrier.
S_INIT_BARRIER	C macro version of s_init_barrier.
s_init_lock	Initialize a lock.
S_INIT_LOCK	C macro version of s_init_lock.
s_lock or s_clock	Lock a lock.
S_LOCK or S_CLOCK	C macro versions of s_lock and s_clock, respectively.
s_unlock	Unlock a lock.
S_UNLOCK	C macro version of s_unlock.
s_wait_barrier	Wait at a barrier.
S_WAIT_BARRIER	C macro version of s_wait_barrier.

5.3.3 Memory Allocation Routines

The memory-allocation routines allow a data-partitioning program to allocate and deallocate shared memory and to change the amount of shared and private memory assigned to a process. Table 5-3 lists the memory-allocation routines in the parallel-programming library.

Table 5-3
Parallel-Programming Library Memory-Allocation Routines

Routine	Description
brk or sbrk	Change private data segment size.
shbrk or shsbrk	Change shared data segment size.
shfree	Deallocate shared data memory.
shmalloc or shrealloc	Allocate shared data memory.

Section 5.5 explains how to use the parallel-programming library routines in a program and Appendix A presents some sample programs. For a detailed reference to the parallel-programming library, refer to Appendix B.

5.4 Analyzing Variable Usage

Before you can convert a loop into a subprogram for data partitioning, you must analyze all the variables in the loop and determine two things:

- Which data can be shared between parallel processes and which data must be local to each parallel process.

- Which variables cause dependencies or *critical sections*, code sections that can yield incorrect results when executed in parallel.

If you have already read Chapter 4, you are familiar with the information presented in this section and you may wish to turn directly to Section 5.5.

5.4.1 Shared Variables and Local Variables

A variable must be local if it is initialized in each loop iteration before it is used. All other variables are shared. Local variables are usually scalar (single-element) variables, although other data structures may be local. On Symmetry systems local variables are declared with the `private` keyword and stored in private memory. When a variable is declared to be private, each process has its own copy of that variable (after a fork) and its value varies from process to process. In contrast, a shared variable can be read or written by any process (after a fork) and all processes access the same memory location for that variable.

On a Symmetry system, a shared variable maps to the same memory cell for each process. For variables allocated in private memory, each process has the same address for a specific variable but, as a result of virtual to physical memory mapping, that address is mapped to a different memory cell.

The following sample matrix multiplication loop contains both shared and local variables. Assume that the outermost loop is the one to be executed in parallel.

```
for (i=0; i<n; i++)
    for (k=0; k<n; k++)
        for (j=0; j<n; j++)
            r[i][j] = r[i][j] + s[i][k] * t[k][j];
```

In this loop, the variables `i`, `k`, and `j` are local: they are initialized at the beginning of each loop iteration before they are used. The variables `r`, `s`, `t`, and `n` are shared. `s`, `t`, and `n` are read-only, and `r` is an array whose index varies directly with the loop index.

Once you have identified the local variables, you can declare variables as shared or private in your program. Table 5-4 lists the mechanisms available in C, C++, and FORTRAN to declare a variable as shared or private.

For Pascal programs, use the **-mp** compiler option to allocate all global variables and all variables allocated at run time to shared memory. All local variables are treated as automatic (stack) variables. The stack may be private or shared.

Table 5-4
Storage-Allocation Mechanisms

Language	Default Storage	Mechanism for Shared Memory	Mechanism for Private Memory
C	private (**–Wc,–Y** option reverses default)	`shared` keyword	`private` keyword
C++	private (**–Wc,–Y** option reverses default)	`shared_t` keyword	`private_t` keyword
FORTRAN	when **–mp** option is specified: shared when **–mp** option is not specified: private	SHARED statement	PRIVATE statement

Special Considerations for Optimization. If you are a C, C++, or FORTRAN programmer, you should be aware that optimization may affect shared memory variables. To ensure correct code for parallel programs, you should declare all shared variables that are accessed or modified by multiple processes, but are *not* protected by a synchronization mechanism, as `volatile`. The compiler treats references to volatile variables and function calls as synchronization points for shared variables. Thus, the compiler optimizes shared memory references only between synchronization points.

If you do not declare a shared variable that will be accessed or changed asynchronously by multiple processes as volatile or protect that variable with a synchronization mechanism, you must ensure that the variables are correctly aligned in memory and that the program is compiled with the **–Wc,–i** option. This forces the compiler to treat all shared variables as volatile regardless of the optimization level. Be aware, however, that using this option produces code with little optimization. Therefore, the execution speed of the program may significantly decrease.

Special Considerations for C Programmers. To declare a variable to be shared or private, simply add the appropriate keyword to the variable's declaration statement. You need to define only static or external variables to be shared or private since automatic variables are handled correctly for you and register variables cannot be shared. By default, external and static variables that are not declared as shared are private. You can reverse this effect by using the **–Wc,–Y** compiler option to specify that all variables allocated at compile time should be placed in shared memory unless they are explicitly declared as private. For more information on the `shared` and `private` keywords, refer to the *DYNIX/ptx C User's Manual*.

Special Considerations for FORTRAN Programmers. As indicated in Table 5-4, you can use the SHARED and PRIVATE statements to declare a variable as shared or private. When programs are compiled with the **–mp** option, all variables are treated as shared except TASK COMMON blocks, variables declared in PRIVATE statements, and variables in a program unit preceded by a `$PRIVATE` directive. If you do not specify the **–mp** option at compile time, all variables are private. For more information about these statements and directives, refer to the *ptx/FORTRAN User's Manual*.

5.4.2 Identifying Dependent Variables

Dependent variables are shared variables that can be read and written by more than one loop iteration. These variables can sometimes pass incorrect information between loop iterations if the iterations are executed out of order or if two loop iterations try to write the variable simultaneously. This section explains how to identify these variables and Section 5.5 presents some special tools and techniques for handling dependent variables to ensure correct results.

You can use the following simple tests to determine whether a shared variable is dependent or independent:

- Is it a *read-only* variable; that is, is it read but never written within the loop?

- Is it an array in which each element is referenced by only one loop iteration? (This can occur when the array index varies directly with the loop index.)

If the answer to either of these questions is "yes," then the variable is independent and you simply declare it as shared. If the answer is "no," then the variable is dependent and you need to determine the type of its dependence.

Dependent variables fall into the following three categories:

- Reduction variables
- Ordered variables
- Locked variables

The remainder of this section explains how to identify these types of dependent variables. Section 5.5.2 describes techniques for handling each type of dependence in your program.

Reduction Variables

A reduction variable is an array or scalar variable that has the following properties:

- It is used in only one associative, commutative operation within the loop. These operations include addition or subtraction, multiplication or division, logical AND, logical OR, and exclusive OR.
- In C, C++, or FORTRAN programs, the operation is of the form:

  var = var op expr

  In C or C++ programs it may also be of the form:

  var op= expr

  In Pascal programs, the operation is of the form:

  var := var op expr

  where *var* is the reduction variable, *op* is an associative, commutative operation, and *expr* is an expression that does not include the variable *var*. The variable may occur in more than one such statement, as long as the operation is the same.

The following loop contains a reduction variable:

```
for (k=0; k<i-1; k++)
    q = q + b[i][k] * w[i-k];
```

In this loop, the variables b, w, and i are independent, because they are read-only within the loop. The variable q is a reduction variable. It is used in a single associative, commutative operation (addition) and the operation has the correct form. Note that the loop index, k, is a local variable.

Shared Ordered Variables

A shared ordered variable is an array or scalar variable that has the following property: the loop consistently yields correct results only if the operations involving the variable are executed (to completion) one iteration at a time, in serial order.

The following example loop contains two shared ordered variables.

```
for (i=0; i < n; i++ ) {
    x[i] = xa[i] + xb[i];
    dx = x[i] - x[i+1];
    y[i] = ya[i] + yb[i];
    dy = y[i] - y[i+1];
    rho[i] = sqrt(dx * dx + dy * dy);
}
```

In this loop, the variables xa, xb, ya, and yb are shared, because they are all read-only. The variables dx and dy are local because they are initialized in each loop iteration before their values are used. The variables x and y are shared ordered since executing the loop iterations in random order would produce different values than when the loop is executed in sequential order.

Shared Locked Variables

A shared locked variable is an array or scalar variable that has the following properties:

- The variable can be read and written by more than one loop iteration.

- If the loop iterations were executed (to completion) one at a time in random order, the operations involving the variable would produce correct results.

The first of these characteristics distinguishes a shared variable from a shared locked variable.

Because a shared locked variable can be read and written by more than one loop iteration and because loop iterations execute simultaneously, we must ensure that only one loop iteration is using the variable at a time. The mechanism to do this is called a lock, hence the name *shared locked variable*.

The following example computes the distance between one city and a number of other cities, then compares each distance with the minimum distance, and selects the array index of the nearest city. This loop contains one locked variable.

```
#define sq(x)    (x) * (x)

x = 0
y = 1
least = 999999.;
for (i=1; i < n; i++) {
    xsqdis = sq(bvrtn[x]-a[i][x]);
    ysqdis = sq(bvrtn[y]-a[i][y]);
    dist   = sqrt(xsqdis + ysqdis);
    if (dist < least) {
        closest = i;
        least   = dist;
    }
}
```

In this loop, the variables bvrtn and a are independent shared variables: they are read-only within the loop. The variables xsqdis, ysqdis, and dist are local: they are written in each iteration before they are read. The variables closest and least must be shared locked. They are read and written by each loop iteration, but the order in which the iterations are executed does not affect the results of the operations involving them. As long as the loop is executed n times, each value of dist is compared with least. As long as nothing changes the value of closest or least between the if statement and either assignment statement, the loop will return the correct answers.

Variable-Analysis Worksheet

As you analyze the variables in your loop, you may find it helpful to use the worksheet shown in in Figure 5-1.

	SHARED	LOCAL	REDUCTION	SHARED ORDERED	SHARED LOCKED
VARIABLE NAME	*Is the variable read-only within the loop OR is it an array where each element is read and written by only one loop iteration?*	*Could the variable be renamed in each iteration without affecting the program result?*	*Is the variable used in only one associative, commutative operation within the loop AND is it always read, then written?*	*If the loop iterations were executed in random order, would the operations involving this variable produce different results?*	*Have you answered "no" to all the other questions?*

Figure 5-1. Variable-analysis worksheet.

To use this worksheet, simply list all the variables in your loop in the first column. For each variable, mark your answers to the listed questions until you either answer "yes" to one question or run out of questions. When you mark a "yes" in any column, you'll find the variable type in the label at the top of the column.

Data Partitioning with DYNIX/ptx

5.5 The Microtasking Program

In a microtasking program, each loop to be executed in parallel is contained in a subprogram which we will call the *looping subprogram*. Section 5.5.1 describes the calling program, Section 5.5.2 describes the looping subprogram, and Section 5.5.3 discusses shared memory allocation.

5.5.1 The Calling Program

The calling program handles the following tasks:

- Including any header files required by the parallel-programming library routines (C and C++ programs only).

- Determining how many parallel processes are created to execute the loop. This determination is based on the number of CPUs in the system. You can either call the parallel-programming library routine **m_set_procs**() or use the default number computed by the parallel-programming library.

- Calling the parallel-programming library routine **m_fork**() to execute each looping subprogram in parallel.

- Optionally, suspending or terminating parallel processes between calls to looping subprograms, and terminating all parallel processes after the last looping subprogram has been executed.

Parallel-Programming Library Header File

DYNIX/ptx includes two C header files that contain declaration statements for the parallel-programming library routines. The file *microtask.h* contains declarations for the microtasking routines and the file *parallel.h* contains declarations for the other routines. Both of these header files reside in the directory */usr/include/parallel*.

C++ versions of *microtask.h* and *parallel.h* exist in */usr/include/CC/parallel*, but are referred to in C++ programs as *<parallel/microtask.h>* and *<parallel/parallel.h>* respectively.

Refer to the parallel-programming man pages in Appendix B for information about which files to include for a specific routine.

5-14

Guide to Parallel Programming
on Sequent Computer Systems

Determining How Many Parallel Processes to Use

To determine how many parallel processes your program will use to execute the loop subprogram, you can either call the parallel-programming library routine **m_set_procs**() or you can use a default number computed by the parallel-programming library. The **m_set_procs**() function sets the number of processes that will exist after subsequent calls to the routine **m_fork**(). If your program uses **m_set_procs**(), you may also want to use the routine **cpus_online**() to find out how many CPUs are currently online.

By default, the number of processes created by **m_fork**() is equal to the number of CPUs online divided by two. By using the **m_set_procs**() function, you can set this number as low as one or as high as the number of CPUs online (**m_set_procs**() deletes 1 from the total number of CPU's online).

In C and C++, the calls to the **cpus_online**() and **m_set_procs**() functions look like this:

```
var = cpus_online();

val = m_set_procs(nprocs);
```

In Pascal, the calls to these functions look like this:

```
var := cpus_online();

val := m_set_procs(nprocs);
```

In FORTRAN, the calls to these functions look like this:

```
var = cpus_online()

val = m_set_procs(nprocs)
```

The variables *var*, *val*, and *nprocs* must all be of type `int` in C and C++ programs, type `integer` in Pascal programs, and type `INTEGER*4` in FORTRAN programs.

You can also use the current value of the **PARALLEL** environment variable to set the number of processes as in the following example:

```
nprocs = getenv("PARALLEL");
```

For more information on **getenv**(), refer to the **getenv**(3C) man page. For more information on the **PARALLEL** environment variable, refer to the **sh**(1) man page.

Calling the Looping Subprogram: The m_fork Routine

The parallel-programming library function **m_fork**() executes the looping
subprogram in parallel. The **m_fork**() function creates processes or reuses a
set of existing processes and assigns them to execute copies of the specified
loop subprogram. It can also pass an argument list to each copy.

In C and C++, the **m_fork**() function call looks like this:

```
m_fork(func[,arg,...]);
```

In FORTRAN, the **m_fork**() function call looks like this:

```
external func
call m_fork(func[,arg,...])
```

In Pascal, use the **p_fork**() function, not the **m_fork**() function:

```
p_fork(func[,arg, ...]);
```

The *func* argument is the name of the looping subprogram and the arguments
specified by *arg* are its parameters. These parameters can be of any type. In
C programs, you must declare the **m_fork**() function to be of type void.

When the **m_fork**() function is called, it determines whether there are
existing child processes, processes created by a previous **m_fork**() call. If
there are existing child processes, it reuses them to execute the loop
subprogram. If not, it creates a new set of child processes to execute the
subprogram.

The **m_fork**() routine creates enough child processes to bring the total
number of processes (including the parent process) to either the default
(number of CPUs online/2) or the number you set with a previous call to the
m_set_procs() function. As **m_fork**() creates child processes, it assigns each
process a private integer variable called *m_myid*, which uniquely identifies
that child process within the set of processes belonging to that program. The
first child process created has the *m_myid* value 0, and so on. You can find
the identification number of any process by calling the parallel-programming
library function **m_get_myid**().

Once child processes are available, **m_fork**() passes them copies of their parameters and starts them executing the looping subprogram *func*. When all the child processes are started, the parent process gives itself a copy of the loop subprogram and parameters, and all the processes execute the loop subprogram until they all return from it. At this point, the child processes spin, waiting for more work. The parent process can either kill the child processes, suspend them, or let them spin until they are reused by another **m_fork** call.

Reusing and Terminating Parallel Processes

As explained previously, a program typically forks as many child processes as it needs at the beginning and does not terminate them until all parallel computation is complete. The parallel-programming library includes three routines to manage child processes after **m_fork**() calls:

- m_park_procs
- m_rele_procs
- m_kill_procs

By default, after the program returns from an **m_fork**() call, the child processes spin, using CPU time. If your program requires a lot of computation before the next **m_fork**() call, it can suspend the child processes and relinquish their CPUs for use by other processes by calling the **m_park_procs**() routine. The program then resumes child process execution by calling the **m_rele_procs**() routine. After the last **m_fork**() call, the program should call the routine **m_kill_procs**() to terminate the child processes.

5.5.2 The Looping Subprogram

This section explains how to construct a looping subprogram. In addition to executing a loop in parallel, the looping subprogram handles the following tasks:

- *Scheduling*, determining which process will execute which loop iterations.

- Protecting code sections that contain dependent variables so that they yield correct results.

- Synchronizing processes as necessary.
- Handling I/O, if required.

Static and Dynamic Scheduling

In data-partitioning programs, you can use either static or dynamic scheduling. Static scheduling requires no communication between processes and is generally used when you know that the computing time is approximately the same for each iteration of your loop. Dynamic scheduling requires more communication, but can even out an unbalanced computing load. In general, dynamic scheduling is used when you know that the computing time varies for each iteration of your loop.

Static Scheduling. A static scheduling algorithm simply divides the loop iterations evenly among the processes. The static scheduling algorithm for a process involves the following steps:

1. Call the parallel-programming library routine **m_get_numprocs**() to determine how many processes were created by the **m_fork**() call. (We'll call this number M.)

2. Call the parallel-programming library routine **m_get_myid**() to find out my process ID number. (We'll call this number N.)

3. Start by executing the Nth loop iteration.

4. Execute every Mth iteration until I reach the end of the loop.

Refer to Appendix A for an sample program that uses static scheduling.

Dynamic Scheduling. With dynamic scheduling, the loop iterations are treated as a task queue, and each process removes one or more iterations from the queue, executes those iterations, and returns for more work. This method is sometimes called "hungry puppies" because the processes "nibble" away at the work until it is all done.

Dynamic scheduling creates more communication overhead than static scheduling because all the processes must access a single shared task queue, but the computing load can be very evenly distributed because no process is idle while there is still work to be done. For data partitioning, the task queue can be implemented by using the **m_next**() routine.

A typical dynamic scheduling algorithm includes the following steps:

1. Lock a lock.

2. Check shared loop index and verify that there is still work to be done.

3. Increment or decrement the shared loop index by *N*. (The **m_next()** routine is useful for this if your shared loop index can start at zero and increment.)

4. Unlock the lock.

5. Execute *N* iterations.

6. Repeat steps 1 through 5 until all the work is finished.

If you use the **m_next()** routine, you do not need to explicitly lock and unlock a lock. These steps are built into **m_next**. Refer to Appendix A for an example program that uses **m_next()** in dynamic scheduling.

Handling Locked Sections

If your loop contains locked variables, you need to use the parallel-programming library routines **m_lock()** and **m_unlock()** to ensure that the code section containing those variables is executed by only one loop iteration at a time. The **m_lock()** call should appear on the line immediately preceding the first reference to a locked variable, and the **m_unlock()** call should appear on the line immediately following the last reference to a locked variable while obeying the block structure of the program.

Refer to Appendix A for an example program that uses these routines to protect the shared loop index in a dynamically scheduled loop subprogram.

The **m_lock()** and **m_unlock()** routines support only one lock per looping subprogram. If your program requires more than one lock at a time, you can use the **s_init_lock()**, **s_lock()** or **s_clock()**, and **s_unlock()** routines. Refer to the **s_lock**(3PPS) man page for more information on these routines.

Handling Reduction Variables

Reduction variables are similar to locked variables, except that you need to protect them with locks only part of the time. You can create a local reduction variable, initialize it within the parallel loop routine, and substitute the local variable name for the reduction variable name throughout the loop. At the end of the loop subprogram, you can call the **m_lock**() function, perform the reduction operation to combine the local reduction variable with the shared reduction variable, and call the **m_unlock**() function. This is more efficient than an ordinary locked variable because each process executes the locked section only once.

For example, consider the following example loop from Section 5.4.2:

```
for (k=mystart; k<end; k+=incr)
    q = q + b[i][k];
```

The reduction variable q is shared. The loop iterations can be executed in any order, but the loop can produce incorrect results if two processes try to read or write q simultaneously. As long as the loop is structured this way, it cannot be executed in parallel. However, if we declare a local variable, lq, each process can add its values of b to lq without affecting any other process. Once each process finishes its calculations, it can lock the shared variable q, add its lq value, and unlock q.

```
lq = 0;
for (k=mystart; k<end; k+=incr)
    lq = lq + b[i][k];
m_lock();
q = q + lq;
m_unlock();
```

Handling Ordered Sections

If your loop contains an ordered variable, you need to ensure that the code sections containing that variable are executed in loop iteration order. To ensure this, repeat the following procedure for each ordered variable in the loop.

1. In the main program, declare the integer variable that will hold the current loop iteration number as volatile. (If the shared ordered variable is named `i`, you might name the new variable something like `iguard`.) Initialize the new variable to the starting value of the loop index.

2. In the looping subprogram, on the line before the first reference to the volatile variable, insert a conditional statement that loops on itself until the loop index value is equal to the value of the iteration count variable.

3. On the line after the last reference to the volatile variable, insert a statement to increment the shared iteration counter variable.

If the ordered variable is written and then read more than once within the loop, you can speed up execution by treating each write and read sequence as a different variable. This allows execution to proceed in parallel between ordered sections.

The following example loop from Section 5.4.2 illustrates these modifications. The shared variables `x` and `y` are ordered. Assume that the programmer has declared two volatile shared variables named `xguard` and `yguard` in the main program and initialized them to zero.

```
nprocs = m_get_numprocs();
for (i=m_get_myid(); i < n-1; i+=nprocs ) {
   while (xguard != i)
      continue;
   x[i] = xa[i] + xb[i];
   dx = x[i] - x[i+1];
   xguard = xguard + 1;
   while (yguard != i)
      continue;
   y[i] = ya[i] + yb[i];
   dy = y[i] - y[i+1];
   yguard = yguard + 1;
   rho[i] = sqrt(dx * dx + dy * dy);
}
```

Synchronizing Processes

A looping subprogram sometimes contains a code section that depends on all
the processes having completed execution of the preceding code. For
example, a looping subprogram might execute more than one loop on the
same set of data, and the algorithm might require that all the processes
finish executing the first loop before starting to execute the second loop. In
such situations, you can set up barriers to synchronize the processes.

The parallel-programming library includes routines to set up two kinds of
barriers. The routine **m_sync()** synchronizes all the processes at a single,
pre-initialized barrier. To set more than one barrier, or to synchronize a
subset of the processes, the looping subprogram can call **s_init_barrier()** to
initialize a barrier and then call **s_wait_barrier()** to synchronize processes
at the barrier.

Handling I/O

Section 2.9 mentioned the complications of doing I/O from the parallel
portion of a program. You can avoid these complications by setting up single-
process sections within a looping subprogram as illustrated by the following
example:

```
m_sync();
if (m_get_myid() == 0) {
    /*  do I/O    */
}
m_sync();
```

The child processes spin while the parent is doing I/O. For more information about programming considerations for I/O, refer to Chapter 7.

5.5.3 Shared Memory Allocation

The parallel-programming library contains a set of routines for dynamic allocation and management of shared memory. For C and Pascal programs, the **shmalloc** and **shfree** routines allocate and release shared memory for data structures whose size is determined at run time. The **shmalloc** routine returns a shared pointer to the newly allocated shared memory.

ptx/C++ does not explicitly support dynamic allocation of shared memory. The default version of the new operator calls **malloc** to allocate private memory. However, you can use the following routine to allocate shared memory at run time:

```
#include <stddef.h>
extern "C" char* shmalloc ( unsigned );
extern void* operator new (size_t size)

{
    return (void*) shmalloc (unsigned (size));
}
```

Assume this routine is contained in the library, *cplus.a*, and the program that dynamically allocates shared memory is called *myprog.C*. To ensure that the linker uses the correct version of the new operator, you must list *cplus.a* before the other libraries as illustrated by the following command:

CC –Wc,–seq myprog.C cplus.a –lpps –lseq

In Pascal, dynamic shared memory allocation is handled by the NEW routine, and FORTRAN does not provide dynamic memory allocation.

The **shbrk** and **shsbrk** routines increase the size of a process's shared data segment and verify that the increase does not cause the shared data segment to overlap the process's shared stack. The parallel-programming library **brk** and **sbrk** routines are used like the standard DYNIX/ptx **brk** and **sbrk** to increase a process's private data segment size, but they also verify that the increase does not cause the private data segment to overlap the process's shared data segment.

5.6 Compiling, Executing, and Debugging

To complete development of your data-partitioned program, follow these steps:

1. Invoke the appropriate compiler with the proper options to link your program with the parallel-programming library.

2. Execute the program and check the results.

3. If necessary, use the DYNIX/ptx parallel symbolic debugger, invoked with the **pdbx** command, to debug the program.

Refer to Appendix A for a listing of sample C, C++, FORTRAN, and Pascal parallel programs.

5.6.1 Compiling the Program

To compile and link a C program, enter the following command:

cc –Wc,–seq *sourcefile*.c **–lpps –lseq**

This command compiles a C source file and links the object code with the parallel-programming library and a Sequent library of special routines to produce an executable file named *a.out*. You can also include the **–g** compiler option to create an executable file that contains debugging information. For more information on these options and other C compiler options, refer to the **cc**(1) man page.

NOTE

If your program contains any variables declared as shared, *you must specify the* **–libpps** *option on the compiler command line.*

To compile and link a C++ program, enter the following command:

CC –Wc,–seq *sourcefile*.C **–lpps –lseq**

This command translates a C++ source file, compiles the output from the C++ translator, and links the object code with the parallel-programming library and a Sequent library of special routines to produce an executable file named *a.out*. You can also include the **–g** compiler option to create an executable file that contains debugging information. For more information on these options and other C++ translator options, refer to the **CC**(1) man page.

To compile and link a Pascal program, enter the following command:

pascal –mp *sourcefile*.p

This command compiles a Pascal source file and links the object code with the parallel-programming library, producing an executable file named *a.out*. It also places all global variables into shared memory. You can also include the **–g** compiler option to create an executable file with debugging information.

For more information on these options and other Pascal compiler options, refer to the *ptx/PASCAL Release Notes*.

To compile and link a FORTRAN program, enter the following command:

fortran –mp *sourcefile.f*

This command compiles a FORTRAN source file and links the object code with the parallel-programming library and a library of special Sequent routines to produce an executable file named *a.out*. You can also include the **–g** compiler option to create an executable file that contains debugging information.

For more information on these options and other FORTRAN compiler options, refer to the **fortran**(1) man page in the man page section of the *ptx/FORTRAN* binder.

For more information on the DYNIX/ptx linker, refer to the **ld**(1) man page in the man page.

5.6.2 Executing the Program

To execute the program, simply enter the name of the executable file from your shell. The default file name is *a.out*.

5.6.3 Debugging the Program

If your program produces incorrect results, you can use the DYNIX/ptx debugger, Pdbx, to isolate any problems. Pdbx is a symbolic debugger based on **dbx**, a debugger widely used in UNIX systems. Use the **pdbx** command to invoke the debugger when debugging parallel programs; otherwise, use the **dbx** command.

When debugging programs that use the parallel-programming library, remember that by default the debugger takes a breakpoint upon exiting from child processes. When the debugger encounters these breakpoints, you must enter Ctrl-Z to return control to the debugger and continue execution. To disable the automatic breakpoint, use the debugger command **ignore exit**.

The parallel-programming library uses the signal **SIGSEGV** to determine when to allocate more space for a process's shared stack. The debugger automatically stops whenever this signal is encountered. To disable these automatic breakpoints, use the command **ignore sigsegv**. For more information on the debugger, refer to the *Pdbx User's Manual*.

Chapter 6

Function Partitioning on Symmetry Systems

Function Partitioning on Symmetry Systems

6.1 Introduction

This chapter describes the Symmetry facilities that support function-partitioning applications. These include facilities for:

- Process creation
- Assignment of processing tasks
- Process synchronization
- Interprocess communication
- Ensuring exclusive access to shared data

This chapter also discusses two simple techniques for function partitioning.

6.2 Models for Function Partitioning

Function partitioning involves creating multiple processes and having them perform different operations on the same data set. The processes may be created within a single program or they may be independent programs created at the operating system level. (DYNIX/ptx system calls linked by pipes are a good example of function partitioning at the operating system level.) The difference between function partitioning at the program level and simple multiprogramming is that the independent processes *cooperate* to solve a single application.

The methods and applications for function partitioning are much too varied to fully describe here. However, we can present two basic techniques for function partitioning: the fork-join technique and the pipeline technique. By using one or a combination of these models, you can solve any function partitioning application.

6.2.1 The Fork-Join Technique

The fork-join technique is appropriate for applications in which no major function requires the results of any other; that is, each major function must be *independent* of the others. For example, consider an application that computes the mean, the mode, and the median of some set of data. None of these calculations depends on the results of either of the others. This application is a good candidate for the fork-join technique.

The algorithm for a fork-join application is:

1. Create a set of processes, giving each one access to a set of shared data. (This step is the fork.)

2. Assign a task to each process.

3. If there is any data that could be changed simultaneously by two or more processes, protect it with a lock.

4. As each process finishes its task, it waits at a barrier until the other processes are finished. (This step is the join.)

5. Proceed with serial execution.

Figure 6-1 illustrates the fork-join programming model.

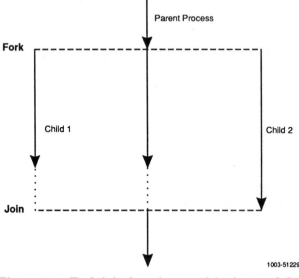

Figure 6-1. Fork-join function-partitioning model.

The following sample code segment illustrates the use of the fork-join technique. Although they are not show here, assume that the functions **get_mean()**, **get_mode()**, and **get_median()** are defined in the source file.

```c
#include <stdio.h>
#include <parallel/microtask.h>
#include <parallel/parallel.h>
#include <sys/types.h>

shared sbarrier_t *barrier;
shared int scores[25];

main()
{
    int avail_procs, nprocs;
    int m_kill_procs(), m_set_procs(), m_get_myid();
    void get_info();

    avail_procs = cpus_online();
    fprintf(stderr, "Number of processors available: %d\n",
        avail_procs);
    fprintf(stderr, "Enter number of processes:");
    scanf("%d",&nprocs);

    if ((m_set_procs(nprocs)) != 0)
        fprintf(stderr,"errno = %d\n",errno);
    s_init_barrier(&barrier,nprocs);
    m_fork(get_info,scores);
    m_kill_procs();
}
void get_info()
{
    int get_mode(),get_median(),get_mean();

    if (m_get_myid() == 0)
        get_mode();
    if (m_get_myid() == 1)
        get_median();
    if (m_get_myid() == 2)
        get_mean();
    }
    s_wait_barrier(&barrier);
/*
 * do further computations with results
 */
}
```

If the additional computation following the call to **s_wait_barrier**() did not exist, the calls to **s_init_barrier**() and **s_wait_barrier**() would not be necessary because entries to and exits from a function are treated as automatic synchronization points.

6.2.2 The Pipeline Technique

The pipeline technique is appropriate for applications in which the major functions depend on each other and the data set or sets are very large. For example, the pipeline technique would be appropriate for a signal-processing application that analyzes satellite data to determine a finite set of categories, assigns each data point to a category, assigns a color value to each data point, and then uses the results to construct a colored image.

The algorithm for a pipelined application is:

1. Create a set of processes, giving each one access to a set of shared data.

2. Assign a task to each process.

3. The first process performs calculations on a portion of the data, writes the results to shared memory, and notifies the next process that the results are available for processing.

4. Assign the first process new data sets and have the next process use the results. Continue in this manner so that each subsequent process uses the results of the previous process until all the work is done.

5. When work runs out, each process terminates or, if there are other tasks to be done, relinquishes its processor or spins until it is assigned a new task.

6. Proceed with serial execution.

Figure 6-2 illustrates the pipeline programming model.

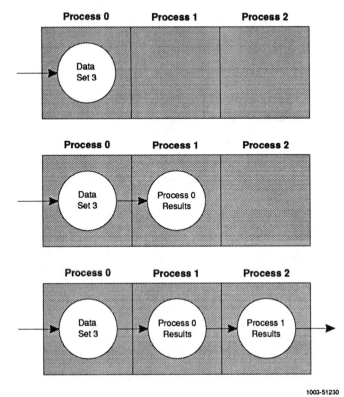

Figure 6-2.   Pipeline function-partitioning model.

6.3 Support for Function Partitioning

The DYNIX/ptx operating system includes system calls or library routines to support process creation, process synchronization, and interprocess communication. Applications that use DYNIX/ptx system calls and the parallel-programming library routines should use other DYNIX/ptx system calls and parallel-programming library routines only and not System V interfaces; these are mutually exclusive sets. The System V interfaces create a new object type with a name space that is inconsistent with the filesystem name space and an access-protection mechanism that is different from that of the file system. Also, these mechanisms don't allow you to extend shared memory, which can be very important in a parallel run-time system. Refer to the *DYNIX/ptx Programmer's Guide* for more information on the System V interfaces. Refer to Appendix B for more information on the parallel-programming library routines.

The ptx/FORTRAN, ptx/PASCAL, ptx/C++, and DYNIX/ptx C compilers provide intercallability between programs and program modules written in different languages. For more information on intercallability, refer to the appropriate compiler manual.

6.3.1 Programming Considerations

When and how the values of shared and private variables are available to different processes has been discussed in both Chapters 5 and 6. You should also be aware of how different processes can communicate by means of automatic variables: if two processes are synchronized, these processes can communicate by passing the address of an automatic variable. The following sample code segments illustrate this point:

```
Process 1                                Process 2

int x;                                   while (!vflag)
private int y    ! automatic variable      printf (*px, *py);
x = 5;
y = 3;
px = &x;
py = &y;
vflag = 1;
```

When process 2 executes, it will display the current value of x, 5, and the current value in the address referenced by the pointer py. Since y is declared as private, the memory cell accessed by the address for y is process dependent.

6.3.2 Process Creation

The **fork**() system call creates a duplicate copy of the current process. In a common type of parallel application on a Symmetry system, the parent process sets up a shared memory region (via **mmap**()) and one or more locks, then forks one or more child processes to share the work. The children inherit the parent's complete memory image, including access to shared memory and locks.

NOTE

*You cannot use both the **fork**() system call and the **m_fork** parallel-programming library routine in the same application.*

*Also, if you use **fork**() to create processes, you should be aware that the stack is private to each process.*

You can use the **cpus_online**() routine to determine how many processors are in the system and available for use. Your application can then determine how many processes to create. If you are the superuser, you may want to use the **tmp_ctl**() system call instead of **cpus_online**(). With this system call you can start up or shut down a processor, return the state of a specific processor, or return the number of configure processors. Refer to the **cpus_online**(3PPS) and **tmp_ctl**(2SEQ) man pages for more information on these routines. For more information on **mmap**(), refer to Chapter 8 and the **mmap**(2SEQ) man page.

6.3.3 Assignment of Processing Tasks

Child processes are identical to the parent. They can be designed to choose their own tasks based on the order of their creation or they can use the **execve**() system call to independently execute new program images. The new image resides in a file that contains either executable object code or a shell script. A child process transformed with an **execve**() never returns to the parent process for new tasks, since the original shared image is destroyed.

6.3.4 Exclusive Access to Files

Certain applications, such as database management systems, require different processes to take turns reading and writing the same files. The **fcntl()** system call provides a mechanism for synchronizing access to a file. The **lockf()** C library routine provides a record locking facility, that is, it provides exclusive access to arbitrary portions of a file. You can also use the parallel-programming library routines **s_lock()** and **s_unlock()** to control access to a file accessed by multiple processes. For more information on these routines, refer to the **s_lock**(3PPS), **fcntl**(2), and **lockf**(3C) man pages.

6.3.5 Synchronization and IPC Using DYNIX Interfaces

This section describes how to synchronize processes using either the parallel-programming library or signals and how to perform interprocess communication (IPC) using shared memory.

Synchronization Using the Parallel-Programming Library

The parallel-programming library routines **s_init_barrier()** and **s_wait_barrier()** initialize a barrier and cause processes to spin until all related processes arrive at the synchronization point, respectively. The program segment in section 6.2.1 shows how to use these two routines.

Synchronization Using Signals

System calls and library routines such as **sigpause()** , **sigvec()**, **sigblock()**, **sigset()**, and **kill()** allow processes to send and receive signals among themselves, and to handle special events such as terminal interrupts. On a Symmetry system, many synchronization tasks in parallel applications can be performed more easily and efficiently using locks and shared variables. However, these standard system calls are still useful for certain situations.

For example, if a child process determines that the parent will not need any help for a significant amount of time, the child can use **sigpause()** to relinquish its processor for use by other applications. When the parent needs the child, the parent can send the child a wake-up signal using **kill()** .

When using signals, take care to avoid race situations in which processes simultaneously signal each other that they are going to sleep and then all go to sleep, waiting on each other for wake-up signals. If the process expects to be without work for only a few milliseconds, it may be more efficient for the process to spin and do nothing rather than relinquish its processor and then reacquire one. Refer to Chapter 7 for more information on this topic.

UNIX Signals on a Multiprocessor. Because a Symmetry system can have multiple processes running simultaneously, some programs that use UNIX signals may behave differently on a Symmetry system than on a uniprocessor. For example, suppose process A sends process B a signal. If there is only one processor, A must have it in order to send the signal, and therefore B must be stopped. B is assured of receiving the signal before executing any more user code. On a Symmetry system, B may be running (on a different processor) when A sends the signal. If B is running user code, A will send B a software interrupt so that B will enter the kernel and see the signal. However, B will execute some small amount of user code between when A sends the signal and when B receives it.

It is also possible for multiple instances of the same signal from different processes to pile up before the signaled process receives them. In this situation, all but one instance of the signal will be lost. For example, if each of N child processes sends a signal to their parent, the parent will not necessarily receive N signals. This type of race condition is also possible on uniprocessors, but may not manifest itself until the program is ported to a multiprocessor.

Interprocess Communication Through Shared Memory

The simplest and most efficient mechanism for interprocess communication is a semaphore in shared memory. In C programs, shared and private data structures are created by using the shared and private keywords; in C++, use the shared_t and private_t keywords. keywords; in C++, use the shared_t and private_t keywords. In Pascal programs, all global and dynamically allocated data is automatically shared when programs are compiled with the **−mp** compiler option. In FORTRAN programs, common blocks can be designated as private by using the TASK COMMON statement, and all static data is automatically shared when the **−mp** option is specified.

To map shared files between processes, you can use the DYNIX/ptx **mmap()** and **munmap()** system calls. The **mmap()** call maps a portion of a file into a process's virtual address space; **munmap()** cancels the mapping. Refer to Chapter 8 for more information on **mmap()**.

6.3.6 Synchronization and IPC Using System V Interfaces

This section describes how to use messages, semaphores, and shared memory using System V interfaces.

Messages

The system calls **msgget()**, **msgsnd()**, **msgctl()**, and **msgrcv()** provide a mechanism for sending and receiving data between processes via message queues. Data can be packaged in messages of arbitrary length. Refer to the **msgget**(2), **msgctl**(2), and **msgop**(2) man pages and the *DYNIX/ptx Programming Guide* for examples and detailed information about these routines.

Semaphores

The **semop()**, **semget()**, and **semctl()** system calls allow programs to create, acquire, release, and delete counting or blocking semaphores. (Counting semaphores are explained in Chapter 2.) The **semop()** system call supports three basic operations:

1. Acquire (lock) one or more instances of the desired resource (such as decrementing the semaphore). The process can either wait (block) or return immediately with an error code if the desired resources are not available.

2. Release (unlock) one or more instances of the desired resource (such as incrementing the semaphore).

3. Wait until the semaphore is zero (or return immediately with an error code if it is not).

For examples and specifications of these system calls, refer to the **semop**(2), **semget**(2), and **semctl**(2) man pages and the *DYNIX/ptx Programming Guide*.

Again, on a Symmetry system many process synchronization tasks can be performed more easily and efficiently using locks and shared variables.

System V Shared Memory Routines

Shared memory can also be controlled using system calls assimilated into DYNIX/ptx from System V as well as those routines described earlier in this chapter. You can use the **shmget()**, **shmctl()**, **shmop()**, **shmat()** system calls to allocate, control, and use shared memory.

Refer to the *DYNIX/ptx Programming Guide* for sample programs and additional information on interprocess communication using System V routines.

Chapter 7

Improving Performance

Figures

Tables

Chapter 7
Improving Performance

7.1 Introduction

This chapter provides information to help you estimate the performance improvement you can expect from using a parallel algorithm on a Symmetry system. It also provides information on how to monitor your parallel application's performance and how to tune both your system and your application for parallel execution.

7.2 Estimating Performance

To estimate the improvement in performance from parallelizing a sequential application, you can use the **prof** utility to determine how much time is spent in different parts of a sequential program and then apply Amdahl's formula to estimate the maximum theoretical speedup that can be gained by converting the program into a program that implements a parallel algorithm. You should also consider how the processes generated by an **m_fork** call should be scheduled across the available hardware. The following three sections provide information about these areas.

7.2.1 The prof Profiler

To determine which subprograms within a program are best suited to parallel execution, use the DYNIX/ptx **prof** utility. The **prof** utility creates a *program execution profile*, a listing that shows you which subprograms (subroutines or functions) account for most of a program's execution time.

To create a **prof** listing, perform the following three steps:

1. Compile a C, C++, Pascal, or FORTRAN program with the profiling option.

2. Execute the program to produce profile data.

3. Run **prof** on the profile data to produce a program execution profile.

To compile a program for profiling, enter the **fortran, pascal, cc**, or **CC** command with the **–p** option, as shown in the following examples:

fortran –p *source_file.f*

pascal –p *source_file*.p

cc –p *source_file*.c

CC –p *source_file*.C

Refer to the *ptx/FORTRAN User's Manual*, the *ptx/PASCAL User's Manual*, the *DYNIX/ptx C User's Manual*, and the *ptx/C++ Release Notes* for more information on these compilers.

Next, execute the compiled program by entering the name of the object file as a command (*a.out* is the default name). As the program is executed, profile data is written to a file called *mon.out*. After execution is completed, enter the following command:

prof

This command uses the information in *mon.out* to create and display a program execution profile at *stdout*. If your application is written in C++, you may want to pipe the output produced by running **prof** through the name demangler and view the final output using **more** by entering the following command:

prof | c++filt

Figure 7-1 shows a portion of a subprogram list from a program execution profile.

%Time	Seconds	Cumsecs	#Calls	msec/call	Name
84.1	81.37	81.37	133874	0.6078	saxpy_
10.7	10.35	91.72	27	383.3	matgen_
2.1	2.04	93.76	26	78.5	sgefa_
1.4	1.37	95.13	2574	0.532	isamax_
1.0	0.92	96.05	2574	0.357	sscal_
0.2	0.16	96.44	26	6.3	sgesl_
0.1	0.14	96.58	28	4.8	fputs
0.1	0.06	96.64	1	60.	smxpy_
0.0	0.03	96.67	1	30.	MAIN_

Figure 7-1. Example subprogram list.

The following information in the subprogram list should be examined:

- The leftmost column, %Time, gives the percentage of execution time used by each subprogram, including the percentage used by each of its subprograms. The subprograms are listed in descending order according to this percentage.

- The fourth column from the left, #Calls, states the number of calls to the subprogram.

- The last column, Name, states the name of the subprogram. In this case, each routine name ends in an underscore character (_) since the program was written in FORTRAN and the ptx/FORTRAN compiler automatically appends an underscore to subprogram names.

From Figure 7-1, you can see that the routine **saxpy** is a good candidate for parallel execution, since it accounts for over 80% of the program execution time and is called 133,874 times.

In C programs, you can also use a macro to identify how much time is spent in a specified area within a function. To do this, you must insert the word "MARK" followed by the name to associate with the code to be timed into your source file. The symbol MARK must be defined before the header file *<prof.h>* either by including the line `define MARK` in your program or by means of a command line argument as in the following example:

cc –p –DMARK foo.c

For more detailed information about **prof**, refer to the **prof**(1) and **prof**(5) man pages.

7.2.2 Amdahl's Equation

Once you have determined which parts of your sequential program are good candidates for parallel execution, you can apply Amdahl's equation to determine the maximum possible speedup that can be gained by converting an ordinary sequential program to a parallel algorithm. This formula should be used as a rule of thumb only, since not all the values in this formula can be accurately determined without actually parallelizing the program. Consider the following values:

T   The amount of (wall clock) time the sequential version of the program takes to execute.

N   The number of processors to dedicate to the parallel version of the program during its execution.

s   The fraction of the execution time T that must be spent in sequential code, such as initialization and I/O. This is usually difficult to estimate accurately, although the **prof** command can be useful in determining what percentage of its time a program spends in each of its subroutines.

For now, assume zero overhead for synchronization and resource contention among the parallel instruction streams. (Information to help you predict the amount of overhead added by switching to a parallel algorithm is provided in the next section.) Assume that all processors will be kept busy doing useful work for the duration of the parallel sections of the code (that is, completely effective dynamic load balancing).

The sequential portion of the program will execute in time

$$s \times T$$

and the parallel portion will execute in time

$$\frac{(1-s) \times T}{N}$$

For example, suppose you have a sequential program that takes 100 minutes to execute and 5% of this time (5 minutes) is spent in sequential code. You parallelize it over 10 processors. Using Amdahl's equation, the total execution time for the parallelized version should be approximately 15 minutes, a 7X speedup:

$$0.05 \times 100 + \frac{0.95 \times 100}{10} = 14.5$$

Many programs spend less than 1% of their time in sequential code. If we use 1% instead of 5% in our formula, the execution time drops to approximately 11 minutes, a 9X speedup:

$$0.01 \times 100 + \frac{0.99 \times 100}{10} = 10.9$$

7.2.3 Processor Availability

Parallel algorithms are simplest and most efficient when they can be based on the following assumption:

Every process has a processor whenever it needs to run.

For example, if you have a 10-processor system, the optimum number of processes for a parallel application is probably 10 or fewer. In practice, however, you should leave enough processors available for other processes so that each process has sufficient resources. In fact, a job that contains more processes than can be kept running simultaneously is likely to encounter the situation illustrated in Figure 7-2. Note that the job will eventually run to completion, but possibly at a great cost to system throughput.

```
Processes 1-9 begin
spinning, waiting for an
event to be posted by
process 10.
                          Process 10 is preempted by
                          process 11 and goes to sleep.

Processes 1-9 keep
spinning, consuming
CPU cycles.
                          Process 10 eventually gets a
                          processor, wakes up, and posts
                          the event.

Processes 1-9 resume.
```

**Figure 7-2. Potential problem due to process/processor
mismatch.**   If the number of processes in a job exceeds the number of
available processors, the situation illustrated here may be encountered.

Under the scheduling algorithm used by DYNIX/ptx, a process runs without
interruption on a processor until one of the following events occurs:

- The process blocks (for example, waits for an I/O operation to be
  completed) or terminates.

- The processor is preempted by another process with greater or equal
  priority.

Also, the lowest priority process that is running user (nonkernel) code is
required to service all interrupts.

Thus, the problem illustrated in Figure 7-2 can be avoided in several ways:

- Leave one or more processors free to execute other jobs and service
  interrupts. (Note that the **m_set_procs**() routine automatically sets
  the number of processes that can be generated by subsequent **mfork**()
  calls to one less than the number of processors online).

- Run the parallel job at a higher priority than other jobs that may be running at the same time. (But you will probably want to leave one processor free anyway.) This option is described in more detail later in this chapter.

- Use a smarter "wait" algorithm, in which a process blocks after spinning for a specified amount of time.

For information on synchronization, refer to Chapter 2.

7.3 Monitoring Performance

The Sequent microsecond clock allows parallel programmers to do fine-grain timing studies of program execution. All Symmetry systems include a clock.

You can map the clock into process address space with the **usclk_init** routine and read the clock with the **getusclk** routine or the C macro, GETUSCLK. On Symmetry systems, overhead for a **getusclk** call is the time required for three instructions to execute (approximately 2 microseconds on a Symmetry Model C) while overhead for GETUSCLK is nil since it does not have the overhead associated with a function call.

For more information on the microsecond clock, refer to the **getusclk(3SEQ)** and **usclk(7)** man pages.

7.4 Tuning for Performance

To improve the performance of your parallel programs, you should consider either modifying the environment in which your parallel programs run or manually optimizing your program. Sections 7.4.1 and 7.4.2 discuss what options are available to you to modify your system to improve the performance of your parallel program. Sections 7.4.3 and 7.4.4 describe several modifications you can make to your code to further optimize your parallel program.

7.4.1 Setting the Environment Type

When the kernel is built, it accesses values in configuration files that determine how the kernel will operate once it is rebuilt and booted. The system configuration file, */etc/conf/uts/symmetry/system.std*, includes a parameter called the environment type. The *environment type* establishes system parameters in accordance with the usage of the machine and must be one of the following values: COMMERCIAL, TIMESHARE, or PARALLEL. The default value of the environment type is TIMESHARE. If your system is primarily used for parallel research and supports less than thirty-two users, you may want to consider setting the environment type to PARALLEL. This setting tunes the kernel to support a 30-process parallel application of multiple processes without swapping due to limited page-table mapping resource. It also results in a small buffer cache since parallel applications typically perform limited I/O operations and have few open files.

If you decide to change your environment type, you must rebuild the kernel. For more information on environment types and rebuilding the kernel, refer to the *DYNIX/ptx System Configuration and Performance Guide.*

7.4.2 Tuning Virtual Memory and Process Priority

If your system is configured for a time-sharing environment (the environment type is TIMESHARE), the two items that can interfere most with performance of parallel applications are excessive paging due to inadequate resident set size and excessive swapping of parallel processes (which can result in the situation described in Figure 7-2). The following sections explain how to tune your Symmetry system to avoid these problems.

Adjusting Resident Set Size

When a program is executed, the operating system assigns it a resident set size. A process's *resident set size* determines the amount of text and data it can maintain in physical memory. The resident set size is based on the disk size of the program's image and other factors. The default minimum resident set size is 64 kilobytes. The default maximum resident size is equal to the amount of memory in the system.

Once the resident set size is determined, pages of text and data are brought into memory as needed until the resident set is filled. At that point, one page must be traded out of the resident set for every page that is brought in. DYNIX/ptx monitors the frequency of these page faults and, if the page fault frequency (pff) is too high, increases the resident set size. If the frequency then becomes too low, the operating system decreases the resident set size. For parallel applications that need periodic access to large data sets, these adjustments can result in periods of frequent page faults and oscillation in the resident set size. They can also cause delays by trading out pages containing locks, thus delaying processes because the locks are not immediately accessible: they are logically accessible, but they are not physically accessible until a page fault occurs. This is transparent to application programs except for the performance loss.

To avoid these problems, you can use the **vmtune** command or the **vm_ctl** system routine to adjust your application's virtual-memory usage parameters, provided that you are the superuser or that your system is configured to allow other users to make such adjustments. If your system is not configured to allow you to change your virtual memory parameters, you may be able to edit the file */etc/conf/uts/kernel/i386_space/param_space.c*, set the proper parameters, and reconfigure the system. To display the current values for most virtual memory parameters, enter the **vmtune** command without parameters.

NOTE

Unlike many system parameters, you cannot use the **config** *utility to change virtual-memory parameters.*

Table 7-1 lists and describes the virtual-memory parameters that are defined in *param_space.c*.

Table 7-1
Virtual-Memory Parameters

Parameter	Description
maxRS, maxRSslop	Together, these parameters control maximum resident set size
root_vm_setrs	Controls whether a nonroot process can call **vm_ctl** to adjust its own resident set size
root_vm_swapable	Controls whether a process can be swapped
root_vm_pffable	Controls whether a process can adjust its page-fault frequency

For more information on these parameters refer to the *DYNIX/ptx System Configuration and Performance Guide* and the **vmtune**(1M) and **vm_ctl**(2SEQ) man pages.

Programs can also use the command prefixes **noswap** and **nopff** to suppress process swapping and adjustment of the process's resident set size based on page-fault frequency. For example, entering the following command suppresses process swapping during execution of the program **m_mult**:

/etc/noswap m_mult

For more information on the command prefixes, refer to the **noage**(1M) man page.

Adjusting Process Priority

Another way to ensure optimal performance for a parallel application is to ensure that its processes have higher scheduling priority than standard applications. You can edit the file */etc/conf/uts/kernel/i386_space/param_space.c* so that a process can set its own priority. The system parameter **root_prio_noage** determines whether a nonroot process can prevent itself from aging. Once the system is properly configured, the following system calls can be used to control the scheduling priority of a process:

- **proc_ctl()** — A privileged process can use this system call to keep its effective priority at a specified level, immune to the scheduling heuristics that tend to favor interactive programs.

- **tmp_affinity()** — A privileged process can use this system call to bind itself to a particular processor. The process will not run on any other processor, and has a higher priority on its chosen processor than any nonbound process. This system call can be used to ensure that all processes in an application have uninterrupted use of their processors, and are not preempted by other applications. (However, because of dynamic load balancing on Symmetry systems, the same effect can be gained simply by assigning the application a high priority using the **nice** command or the **nice()** system call, possibly in conjunction with the **proc_ctl** system call.)

Many of the capabilities provided by these system calls can be accessed using the following DYNIX/ptx command prefixes:

- **noage** — Suppress adjustment of the process's priority

- **nice** — Adjust the process's priority

- **onproc** — Run the process on the specified processor

For example, the following command line runs the command **grindaway** on processor 1, with aging suppressed and its priority increased by 10 (the lower the **nice** value, the higher the priority):

nice --10 /etc/onproc 1 /etc/noage **grindaway**

Refer to the **nice**(1), **nice**(2), and **noage**(1M) man pages for details.

Cautions

Overuse of priority and resident set size adjustment can lead to system deadlock. If both **noswap** and **nopff** are specified, you could create a nonswappable process that deadlocks the system by consuming most of physical memory. If both **noage** and **nice** are used, a single program could hang the system by using all the processors and then getting into an infinite loop.

7.4.3 Optimizing Your Program for Performance

This section describes some techniques that may help you to further improve the execution speed of your program.

NOTE

Benchmark programs present some special tuning problems because they often use large data sets but involve less computation than real applications, so the overhead of paging the data into memory may account for most of the execution time. If you suspect this problem, try executing parallel sections more than once. After the first execution, the data will have been paged into memory, so subsequent repetitions will not have paging overhead.

Renaming Variables

Renaming variables is a technique that can be used to shorten locked or ordered loop sections, thereby increasing the portion of the loop that can be executed in parallel. To determine whether a loop can benefit from this technique, start at the end of the loop and examine each reference to the locked or ordered variable until you find the last statement where it is assigned a value. If this is not the last reference to the variable, declare a new local variable, assign it the value of the shared locked or shared ordered variable, and substitute the local copy throughout the rest of the loop.

Ensuring Successive Memory References

Unnecessary paging can result when a parallel process must use data scattered among different pages of memory. For best results, try to structure programs so that each parallel process works with a page of data at a time. For matrix operations in FORTRAN programs, you can do this by making each parallel process work with one column of data at a time. For matrix operations in C, C++, and Pascal programs, make each process work with one row of data at a time. For FORTRAN DO loops without ordered sections, set the CHUNK parameter to N, a value that evenly divides the work among the available processors so that N number of consecutive iterations are executed on the same processor.

7.4.4 Input/Output

I/O in parallel programs is complicated by two factors:

- Multiple processes writing to the same file may cause unpredictable results since each DYNIX/ptx process maintains a table of its open own files

- There is a tendency for a process to block (relinquish its processor) during an I/O operation

To improve performance of your parallel application by eliminating the overhead generated by these two factors, you should follow the following guidelines:

- As much as possible, perform I/O only while a single process is active. If possible, complete all reads before spawning any child processes and delay all writes until after all children have terminated.

- If it is necessary to perform I/O while multiple processes are active, have one process act as a server to perform all I/O. Use multiple I/O buffers or message buffers, if necessary, to allow the other processes to continue while the I/O server is blocked.

- If all processes must perform I/O, have them write to different files if this is convenient.

- If two or more processes must write to the same sequential file, use the O_APPEND flag of the **fcntl**() system call (see **fcntl**(2) and **fcntl**(5)) to ensure that each write occurs at the end of the file.

- If two or more processes must read or write the same direct-access file (using the **lseek**() system call followed by **read**() or **write**()), place both the **lseek**() call and the subsequent **read**() or **write**() call in the same critical region.

Chapter 8
Advanced Techniques

Figures

Chapter 8
Advanced Techniques

8.1 Introduction

This chapter provides more detail on shared memory and locking mechanisms for readers who are interested in bypassing the parallel-programming library to either design their own parallel-programming support package or to control shared memory access. This chapter describes how to use the **mmap**() system call and locks to share memory among multiple processes. (For more information on the Symmetry architecture, refer to the *Symmetry Multiprocessor Architecture Overview* or the *S3 System Summary*.)

The DYNIX/ptx operating system allows two or more processes to share a common region of system memory. Any process with access to a shared memory region can read or write in that region in the same way that it reads or writes in ordinary memory. Access to shared memory is controlled by the **mmap**() system call.

To help ensure that one process does not modify a shared data structure while another process is using it, Sequent systems provide hardware locking mechanisms. On Symmetry systems, single-byte load and store operations are always atomic (indivisible), as are 16- and 32-bit loads and stores that are aligned on natural boundaries. To ensure that any other operation is executed atomically, you must protect it with a locking routine using the Symmetry locking mechanism. For Symmetry systems, locking is handled by special system bus and cache protocols. The locking mechanism is invoked with a special prefix to certain Symmetry assembly language instructions.

8.2 Mapping Shared Memory

The **mmap**(2) man page is a detailed specification of the **mmap**() system call, upon which the DYNIX/ptx shared-memory implementation is based. In general, **mmap**() can be used to map a portion of any file or any region of the system's physical address space into a process's virtual address space. A process creates a shared-memory region by opening an ordinary file, then using **mmap**() to map the file into the process's virtual address space. If the high end of the mapped region is above the current program "break" (as returned by the **sbrk**() system call), the "break" is set to the high end of the mapped region. However, any memory between the old break and the low end of the mapped region is inaccessible unless it is memory-mapped by a subsequent call to **mmap**.

A shared-memory allocator analogous to **malloc** (see **malloc**(3) man page) can be built using **mmap** to acquire needed memory in the same way that **malloc**() uses **sbrk**(). In fact, the parallel-programming library routines **shmalloc**(), **shbrk**(), and **shsbrk**() use **mmap**() in this way.

NOTE

To prevent overwriting previously mapped pages, calls to **mmap** *should occur consecutively without interleaving calls which themselves reference routines that map data including* **sbrk**, **shmalloc**, *and any FORTRAN I/O statements.*

Mapped regions created with **mmap**() are inherited (shared) by the process's children. Thus, in an application involving a parent process and one or more identical (not exec-ed) children, the parent first maps the necessary shared memory, initializes any locks or other shared variables, then forks the children. (The run-time start-up routine, **_start**, handles initialization of shared memory by calling the **_ppinit**() routine before calling a program's **main**() routine. This routine maps the program's shared data segment into shared memory and performs miscellaneous run-time initialization for other library routines.) Unrelated processes can also share memory by independently mapping the same file into their virtual memory .

Note, however, that **mmap**() affects only the calling process and any **subsequently** forked children. If child process A expands its shared-memory region, the expansion will not show up in its sibling process, B. If B tries to access a variable set up by A in the new portion of A's address space, B will receive a **SIGSEGV** (segmentation fault) signal. Of course, B can catch this signal and use it as an indication that B needs to grow its own shared-memory region to match A's. This mechanism is used by the parallel-programming library to keep all processes' shared-memory regions up to date.

Specifying Locations of Memory Segments

You can control the gap between the private data segment and the shared data segment by using linker directives that specify the location of memory segments. The file containing these directives is typically called an *ifile*. This file can be specified on the compile command line or at link time. For more information on these directives, refer to the *DYNIX/ptx ld User's Guide*.

Mapped Files

The parallel-programming library immediately unlinks the temporary file that it uses to create the shared memory region. (The disk space associated with the temporary file is not released until the file is closed.) However, there are many ways to use the file that is mapped into a shared-memory region:

- The file acts like a paging area for the mapped memory region. The memory contents are copied out to the file when the process is swapped or when it exits, or when the region is otherwise unmapped by the last process that has it mapped. Thus, the file can be useful in post-mortems.

- If the mapped portion of the file already exists when the file is mapped, the contents of the file are immediately available "in memory." (Technically, the contents are paged in as they are needed.) Thus, a previously obtained snapshot of shared memory can be easily restored.

- An application-specific monitor or debugger can plug into an executing parallel application by mapping the application's mapped file into its own address space.

- **read()** and **write()** operations to the mapped regions of the file also affect the corresponding memory. Thus, ordinary utilities such as **cp** can be used to capture the contents of shared memory.

Note, however, that a file cannot be truncated while it is mapped. Thus, entering the following command will not work:

cp saved_mem mapped_file

Also note that if you map a file whose size is not an integral multiple of the file system block size (usually 8192), **mmap**() will pad the file with null bytes to the end of the block. If you do not have write access to the file, **mmap**() will fail.

Mapping Shared Memory from Unrelated Processes

Creating shared files is a three-part process:

1. Set up your main program or programs to explicitly call a subprogram that initializes shared memory.

2. Set up the subprogram to call **mmap** and initialize shared files.

3. Set up a file of assembler directives or a file of linker commands that define the starting address of each shared file.

The following pages contain an example showing how to use the **mmap** system call to create shared memory for unrelated processes. The example illustrates two techniques. The first technique is to use the assembler to locate the shared data and the second is to use the linker to locate the shared data. Note that the example illustrates these techniques for a single shared file. To create multiple shared files, edit the subprogram that initializes shared memory to open each file and to call **mmap** using the file descriptor returned from the **open** call. You must also add assembler directives or linker commands to define the starting address for each shared file.

NOTE

These examples do not use a full pathname for the shared file, so they must be executed in the same directory.

Using the Assembler to Locate Shared Data. The following two FORTRAN programs declare the common block SHARED, call the subroutine FINIT to initialize shared memory, and then take turns writing values to the shared file. The first program, *x1.f*, waits for the other program to write the shared variable A, writes the shared variable B, waits for the other program to write C, and then exits.

```
      COMMON /SHARED/ _START,A,B,C,_END
      INTEGER*4 _START,A,B,C,_END

      EXTERNAL FINIT

      CALL FINIT(_START,_END)

      WRITE(6,10)
   10 FORMAT( 12H WAIT FOR A )

   20 CONTINUE
      IF ( A .NE. 1 ) GOTO 20

      WRITE(6,30)
   30 FORMAT( 9H WRITE B )

      B = 1

      WRITE(6,40)
   40 FORMAT( 12H WAIT FOR C )

   50 CONTINUE
      IF ( C .NE. 1 ) GOTO 50

      STOP
      END
```

The second program, *x2.f*, initializes itself in the same way as *x1.f*. It then writes the shared variable A, waits for the other program to write the shared variable B, writes the shared variable C, and exits.

```
        COMMON /SHARED/ _START,A,B,C,_END
        INTEGER*4 _START,A,B,C,_END

        EXTERNAL FINIT

        CALL FINIT(_START, _END)

        WRITE(6,10)
10      FORMAT( 9H WRITE A )

        A = 1

        WRITE(6,20)
20      FORMAT( 12H WAIT FOR B )

30      CONTINUE
        IF ( B .NE. 1 ) GOTO 30

        WRITE(6,40)
40      FORMAT( 9H WRITE C )

        C = 1

        STOP
        END
```

The following file, *finit.c*, initializes the shared file and rounds the size of the shared memory segment up to the nearest page boundary.

```
/*
 * finit()
 *   Parallel run-time start-up routine.
 */
#include <a.out.h>
#include <string.h>
#include <sys/errno.h>
#include <sys/ioctl.h>
#include <sys/fcntl.h>
#include <sys/types.h>
#include <sys/file.h>
#include <sys/mman.h>
#include <sys/pmap.h>
#include "parc.h"

extern int errno;
int _pgoff;

finit_(start, end)
    char *start, *end;
{
    int fd, szshared;

    printf("start %x, end %x\n", start, end);
    fd = open("SHARED_FILE", O_RDWR|O_CREAT, 0666);
    if (fd < 0)
        bad_init("open", errno);

    _pgoff = getpagesize() - 1;

    szshared = (int) PGRND(end - start);
    if (MMAP(fd, start, szshared, 0) < 0)
        bad_init("mmap", errno);
}
/*
 * bad_init()
 *   For some reason, couldn't init --
 *   complain and exit with error status.
 */

static bad_init(msg, err)
    char *msg;
    int err;
{
    perror(msg);
    _exit(err);
}
```

The header file *parc.h* defines the MMAP and PGRND macros used in *finit.c*.

```
/*
 * parc.h
 *   Parallel C support library definitions.
 */

/*
 * MMAP() is shorthand for calling mmap().
 */

#define  MMAP(fd,va,sz,pos)    \
    mmap(va, sz, PROT_RDWR, MAP_SHARED, fd, pos)
/*
 * PGRND() rounds up a value to next page boundary.
 */
#define  PGRND(x) (char *) (((int)(x) + _pgoff) & ~_pgoff)
```

The following assembly language file, *x.s*, sets the base address of the SHARED common block:

```
.globl  shared_
.set    shared_,0x100000
```

Note that the name of the common block is in lower case and is followed by the underscore character (_). The ptx/FORTRAN compiler automatically converts all variable names to lowercase unless the **–case** or **–commoncase** command-line options are specified. The compiler also automatically adds an underscore to routine and common block names.

The following *makefile* compiles, links, and executes the various sections of this application. Note that the characters $& precede the prerequisites for the target all to indicate that *x1.f* and *x2.f* can be compiled in parallel. For more information on the parallel support capability of the **make** utility, refer to the **make**(1) man page.

```
all: $& x1 x2
x1 : x1.f x.o finit.o
    fortran -o x1 x1.f x.o finit.o

x2 : x2.f x.o finit.o
    fortran -o x2 x2.f x.o finit.o
x.o: x.s

finit.o  :
    cc -c finit.c

clean :
    rm -f x1 x2 *.o SHARED_FILE

run :
    rm -f SHARED_FILE
    ./x1 & ./x2 &
```

Using the Linker to Locate Shared Data. You can replace the file of assembler directives with a file of linker directives. The file of linker directives for this example contains a single line:

```
shared_=0x100000;
```

Modifying the makefile to use an *ifile* (the file containing linker directives) results in the following:

```
all: $& x1 x2
x1 : x1.f finit.o
    fortran -o x1 x1.f finit.o ifile

x2 : x2.f finit.o
    fortran -o x2 x2.f finit.o

finit.o  :
    cc -c finit.c

clean :
    rm -f x1 x2 *.o SHARED_FILE

run:
    rm -f SHARED_FILE
    ./x1 & ./x2 &
```

8.3 Locked Instructions

The Symmetry locking mechanism uses bytes of memory as locks. Any byte of memory can be used as a lock. A lock's least significant bit determines its state: locked (1) or unlocked (0). Reading a lock returns the state of this bit (0 or 1) and then sets it automatically to 1, thereby locking the lock. This operation is indivisible, or *atomic*. Writing a 0 to a lock location clears the lock. For a backoff reference lock, the remaining bits are used to determine and set the delay before attempting another lock.

Symmetry locking and unlocking routines typically use the XCHG instruction to perform atomic test-and-set and test-and-clear operations.

8.3.1 The LOCK Prefix

Since locking is handled by the system bus hardware, locking mechanisms are implemented in assembly language. These can be included in C programs as asm functions (also referred to as asm macros). For information on asm functions, refer to the *DYNIX/ptx C User's Manual*. They can also be implemented as out-of-line locking routines such as **s_lock()** and **s_unlock()**. (Refer to Chapter 5 for more information on these routines.)

To set the bus lock, precede an assembly instruction with the LOCK prefix. This prefix assures the atomicity of the instruction that it prefixes. The LOCK prefix can be used with the following assembler instructions for 8-, 16-, and 32-bit operations:

```
ADD   ADC   AND   BT    BTS   BTR   BTC   INC
NEG   NOT   OR    SBB   SUB   XCHG  XOR
```

Refer to the *DYNIX/ptx Assembly Language User's Manual* for more detailed information on these instructions.

NOTE

The XCHG instruction is always locked, whether it is preceded by the LOCK prefix or not.

8.3.2 Sample Lock and Unlock Routines

The following locking routines should be studied carefully before writing your own lock and unlock routines. These routines were designed for efficient execution on a Symmetry system. The first lock, the backoff reference, is designed for use when contention for multiple locks is common. Because of its low bus utilization, more bus bandwith remains for processes that are not contending for a specific lock. The second lock, the queue lock, is more efficient in situations where there are a large number of processes contending for a lock.

Figure 8-1 illustrates the performance of these locks on a Symmetry System.

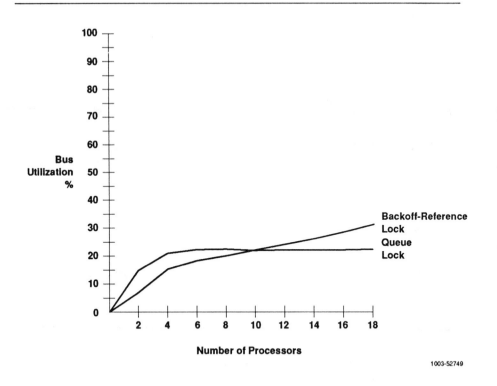

Figure 8-1. Bus utilization of backoff reference and queue locks.

To use the asm functions that follow in your parallel application, copy the file
/usr/include/parallel/parallel.h into your directory and replace the
functions S_INIT_LOCK, S_LOCK, S_CLOCK, and S_UNLOCK with one of
the function groups described below. Then, reference the new version of
parallel.h in your source file with the #include directive.

Low- to Moderate-Contention Lock (Backoff Reference)

The following versions of the asm functions S_INIT_LOCK, S_LOCK,
S_CLOCK, and S_UNLOCK have been coded for use when contention for
multiple locks is common. The algorithms used by these functions are based
on T.E. Anderson's work on locks as described in his paper "The Performance
of Spin Lock Alternatives for Shared-Memory Multiprocessors" (see
Bibliography).

The asm macro S_INIT_LOCK initializes a memory-based lock:

```
#define S_INIT_LOCK(lp)   *lp = L_UNLOCKED; if (!usclk_base) usclk_init()
```

The S_INIT_LOCK macro is similar to the version in the parallel-programming library in that both versions initialize a memory-based lock by setting the address pointed to by `lp` to zero. The difference is that the version presented here also initializes the microsecond clock.

After the lock is initialized, it can be locked with the S_LOCK or S_CLOCK routines. (Remember that the difference between these two functions is that S_LOCK spins until it acquires the lock and S_CLOCK is only successful if the lock is free.) The versions of S_LOCK and S_CLOCK that follow use the XCHG instruction to perform atomic test-and-set and test-and-clear operations as do the versions in the parallel-programming library. Because a lock is an implicit part of the XCHG instruction, the LOCK prefix is unnecessary. In contrast to the versions in the parallel-programming library, these lock routines use the microsecond clock to poll the lock and that the polling rate adjusts exponentially to the number of processes. In addition, the lock remembers the polling rate of the last process to obtain the lock. Using this algorithm, locking the lock is only attempted when there is a higher probability that the lock is available.

```
typedef unsigned char slock_t;        /* 's' for "spin"-lock */

#define L_UNLOCKED    0
#define L_LOCKED      1

/*
 * Was a conditional lock request granted (L_SUCCESS) or denied (L_FAILED) ?
 */
#define L_SUCCESS     1
#define L_FAILED      0

asm void S_LOCK(laddr)
{
%reg laddr; lab delay, wait, try, done;
    movb    (laddr),%al       /* start with a polling rate of half */
    orb     $2,%al            /* force low bit on initially */
    shrb    $1,%al            /* halve the polling rate and check for locked */
    jc      delay             /* if locked, don't disturb it */
```

```
try:
    xchgb   %al,(laddr)        /* attempt the lock */
    testb   $1,%al             /* did we get it? */
    je      done               /* if so, done */
    stc                        /* another process got it--increase delay */
    rclb    $1,%al             /* double the polling rate plus 1 */
    andb    $127,%al           /* limit polling rate to tolerable level */
delay: subl  %edx,%edx         /* delay %al microseconds */
    addb    $89,%ah            /* increment by prime number */
    movb    %ah,%dl            /* to choose new number */
    andb    %al,%dl            /* limit to max delay */
    movl    _usclk_base,%ecx
    addl    (%ecx),%edx
wait: cmpl   (%ecx),%edx
    jns     wait               /* watch out for wraparound (don't use jl) */
    testb   $1,(laddr)         /* poll the lock */
    je      try                /* if free, attempt to obtain it */
    jmp     delay              /* poll again later */
done:
%mem laddr; lab delay, wait, try, done;
    movl    laddr,%ecx
    movb    (%ecx),%al
    orb     $2,%al
    shrb    $1,%al
    jc      delay
try:
    xchgb   %al,(%ecx)
    testb   $1,%al
    je      done
    stc
    rclb    $1,%al
    andb    $127,%al
delay: subl  %edx,%edx
    pushl   %ecx
    addb    $89,%ah            /* increment by prime number */
    movb    %ah,%dl            /* to choose new number */
    andb    %al,%dl            /* limit to max delay */
    movl    _usclk_base,%ecx
    addl    (%ecx),%edx
wait: cmpl   (%ecx),%edx
    jns     wait
    popl    %ecx
    testb   $1,(%ecx)
    je      try
    jmp     delay
done:
}
```

The following is the code for the S_CLOCK operation:

```
asm S_CLOCK(laddr)
{
%reg laddr; lab done;
    movb    $L_LOCKED, %dl
    movl    $L_SUCCESS, %eax
    xchgb   %dl, (laddr)      /* test and set lock */
    testb   $L_LOCKED,%dl     /* if we got it, return success */
    jne     done
    movl    $L_FAILED, %eax   /* else return failure */
done:
%mem laddr; lab done;
    movb    $L_LOCKED, %dl
    movl    laddr, %ecx
    movl    $L_SUCCESS, %eax
    xchgb   %dl, (%ecx)       /* test and set lock */
    testb   $L_LOCKED, %dl    /* if we got it, return success */
    jne     done
    movl    $L_FAILED, %eax   /* else return failure */
done:
}
```

The S_UNLOCK routine unlocks a lock. The following is the code for the unlock operation:

```
asm void S_UNLOCK(laddr)
{
%reg laddr;
    movb    $0xfe, %al
    lock    andb %al, (laddr) /* clear lock, "atomically" */
%mem laddr;
    movb    0xfe, %al
    movl    laddr, %ecx
    lock    andb %al, (%ecx)  /* clear lock, "atomically" */
}
```

High-Contention Lock (Queue Lock)

The asm functions X_LOCK, X_UNLOCK, and X_INIT_LOCK provide the functionality of a queue lock. A queue lock provides the best execution time and can be implemented for an infinite number of processes. Until the number of processes exceeds 16, the queue lock creates more traffic on the bus than a backoff reference lock.

Each lock requires 5 bytes of memory and each process competing for the lock must allocate a one-byte structure for use when competing for the lock. This byte must be allocated at an even address, and bus contention will result if multiple processes allocate their bytes in the same cache block.

The lock structure that must be aligned to a 4-byte boundary is:

```
struct lock {
    int q;
    char l;
};
```

The following is the code for the asm functions X_INIT_LOCK, X_LOCK, and X_UNLOCK.

```
/*
 * To initialize the lock at (%ecx):
 */
void asm X_INIT_LOCK(lock)
{
%reg lock;
    leal    4(lock),%eax
    movl    %eax,(lock)
    movb    $1,(%eax)
%mem lock;
    movl    lock,%ecx
    leal    4(%ecx),%eax
    movl    %eax,(%ecx)
    movb    $1,(%eax)
}


/*
 * To get the lock at (base), use mycell at even
 * address mycell:
 */
void asm X_LOCK(base, mycell)
{
%reg base, mycell; lab spin;
    movl    mycell,%eax
    movb    $1,%dl
    andb    (%eax),%dl      # low bit is the current cell value
    orb     %dl,%al
    xchgl   %eax,(base)     # get into the queue
    movb    $1,%dl
    andb    %al,%dl         # get the process in front of me's bit value
    xorb    %dl,%al         # clear the value bit--leaving only the addr
spin: cmpb %dl,(%eax)       # is the lock clear?
    je      spin
```

```
%mem base, mycell; lab spin;
    movl    mycell,%eax
    movl    base,%ecx
    movb    $1,%dl
    andb    (%eax),%dl      # low bit is the current cell value
    orb     %dl,%al
    xchgl   %eax,(%ecx)     # get into the queue
    movb    $1,%dl
    andb    %al,%dl         # get the process in front of me's bit value
    xorb    %dl,%al         # clear the value bit--leaving only the addr
spin: cmpb  %dl,(%eax)      # is the lock clear?
    je      spin
}

/*
 *  To unlock:
 *  xorb    $1,mycell       # the bit is changed--unlocked
 */
void asm X_UNLOCK(mycell)
{
%reg mycell;
    xorb    $1,(mycell)
%mem mycell;
    movl    mycell,%ecx
    xorb    $1,(%ecx)
}
```

For more information on these locks, refer to the paper "An Analysis of
Synchronization Algorithms for Shared Memory Multiprocessors," by G.
Graunke and S. Thakkar (see *Bibliography*).

Appendix A
Program Examples

Appendix A
Program Examples

A.1 Introduction

This appendix lists C, C++, FORTRAN, and Pascal data partitioning programming examples.

A.2 C Examples

This section contains three data partitioning examples coded in C. These examples were compiled and executed on a Symmetry system running DYNIX/ptx 1.2 and on a Symmetry system running DYNIX 3.1.

Static Scheduling

```
/*
 * Multiply two matrices, store results in third matrix,
 * and print results.
 *
 * To compile under DYNIX/ptx: cc -Wc,-seq -o cstatic cstatic.c -lpps -lseq
 * To compile under DYNIX:     atscc -o cstatic cstatic.c -lpps
 *
 */

#include <stdio.h>                 /* standard I/O header */
#include <parallel/microtask.h>    /* microtasking header */
#include <parallel/parallel.h>     /* parallel library header */

#define SIZE 10                    /* size of matrices */

/* Global (shared memory) data */

shared float a[SIZE][SIZE];        /* first array */
shared float b[SIZE][SIZE];        /* second array */
shared float c[SIZE][SIZE];        /* result array */

main()
{
    void init_matrix(), m_fork(), m_kill_procs(), matmul(), print_mats();
    int nprocs;                    /* number of parallel processes */
    int avail_procs;               /* number of available processors */
```

```
    avail_procs = cpus_online();
    fprintf(stderr,"Number of processors available: %d\n",avail_procs);
    fprintf(stderr,"Enter number of processes:");
    scanf("%d",&nprocs);

    init_matrix(a, b);            /* initialize data */
    m_set_procs(nprocs);          /* set # of processes */
/*
 * Include the next line if running DYNIX to flush standard
 * error.  This is done automatically for you under DYNIX/ptx.
 *
 * fflush(stderr);
 *
 */

    m_fork(matmul, a, b, c);      /* execute parallel loop */
    m_kill_procs();               /* kill child processes */
    print_mats(a, b, c);          /* print results */
}


/* initialize matrix function */

void init_matrix(a, b)
float a[][SIZE], b[][SIZE];
{
    int i, j;

    for (i = 0; i < SIZE; i++) {
        for (j = 0; j < SIZE; j++) {
            a[i][j] = (float)i + j;
            b[i][j] = (float)i - j;
        }
    }
}


/* matrix multiply function */

void matmul(a, b, c)
float a[][SIZE], b[][SIZE], c[][SIZE];
{
    int i, j, k, nprocs;

    nprocs = m_get_numprocs();          /* no. of processes */
```

```
    for (i = m_get_myid(); i < SIZE; i += nprocs) {
        for (j = 0; j < SIZE; j++) {
            for (k = 0; k < SIZE; k++)
                c[i][k] += a[i][j] * b[j][k];
        }
    }
}


/* print results function */

void print_mats(a, b, c)
float a[][SIZE], b[][SIZE], c[][SIZE];
{
    int i, j;

    for (i = 0; i < SIZE; i++) {
        for (j = 0; j < SIZE; j++) {
            printf("\ta[%d][%d] = %3.2f\tb[%d][%d] = %3.2f",
                i, j, a[i][j], i, j, b[i][j]);
            printf("\tc[%d][%d] = %3.2f\n", i, j, c[i][j]);
        }
    }
}
```

Dynamic Scheduling

```
/*
 * Use Cartesian coordinates to find the city closest to
 * Beaverton, Oregon, and print the name and distance
 * from Beaverton.
 *
 * To compile under DYNIX/ptx: cc -Wc,-seq -o cdynamic cdynamic.c -lpps
 *          -lm -lseq
 * To compile under DYNIX:     atscc -o cdynamic cdynamic.c -lpps -lm
 *
 */


#include <stdio.h>                   /* standard I/O header */
#include <math.h>                    /* math library header */
#include <parallel/microtask.h>     /* microtasking header */
#include <parallel/parallel.h>      /* parallel library header */

#define NCITIES 10                  /* number of cities */
#define BITE 1                      /* bite of work */
```

```
/* Global (shared memory) data */

shared float shortest;              /* distance to nearest city */
shared int closest;                 /* index of nearest city */

struct location {
    char *name;
    float x, y;
};

shared struct location cities[NCITIES] = {
    { "CHICAGO", 2000., 100. },
    { "DENVER", 500., -550. },
    { "NEW YORK", 150., 100. },
    { "SEATTLE", 0., 200. },
    { "MIAMI", 3500., -2000. },
    { "SAN FRANCISCO", -100., -1000. },
    { "RENO", 200., -600. },
    { "PORTLAND", -17., 0.  },
    { "WASHINGTON D.C.", 3000., -400. },
    { "TILLAMOOK", -70., -50. },
};

shared struct location beaverton = { "BEAVERTON", 0., 0. };

main()
{
    void get_cities(), find_dis(), m_fork();
    shortest = 999999999.;

    m_fork(find_dis, cities);
    printf("%s is closest to Beaverton.\n",
      cities[closest].name);
    printf("%s is %3.2f miles from Beaverton.\n",
      cities[closest].name, shortest);
}


/* find distance to nearest city */

void find_dis(cities)
struct location cities[];
{
    int i, base, top;    /* local loop index, start & end value */
    float xsqdis, ysqdis, dist;
```

```
      while ((base = BITE*(m_next( )-1)) < NCITIES) {
          top = base + BITE;              /* take a bite of work */
          if (top >= NCITIES) top = NCITIES-1;

          /* execute all iterations in bite of work */

          for (i = base; i < top; i++) {
              xsqdis = pow(fabs(beaverton.x - cities[i].x),2.);
              ysqdis = pow(fabs(beaverton.y - cities[i].y),2.);
              dist   = sqrt(xsqdis + ysqdis);
              m_lock();
              if (dist < shortest) {
                  closest = i;
                  shortest = dist;
              }
              m_unlock();
          }
      }
}
```

Dynamic Shared Memory Allocation

```
/*
 * Multiply two matrices, store results in third
 * matrix, and print results
 *
 * to compile under DYNIX/ptx: cc -Wc,-seq -o shmem shmem.c -lpps -lseq
 * to compile under DYNIX:     atscc -o shmem shmem.c -lpps
 *
 */


#include <stdio.h>                      /* standard I/O header */
#include <parallel/microtask.h>        /* microtasking header */
#include <parallel/parallel.h>         /* parallel library header */

/* Global (shared memory) data */

shared float **a;                       /* first array */
shared float **b;                       /* second array */
shared float **c;                       /* result array */
```

```
main()
{
    char *shmalloc();
    float **setup_matrix();
    void init_matrix(), m_fork(), m_kill_procs(), matmul(), print_mats();
    int size ;/* loop end value and loop increment */

    fprintf(stderr,"Enter array size:");
    scanf("%d",&size);

    a = setup_matrix (size, size);/* allocate shared */
    b = setup_matrix (size, size);/*       memory     */
    c = setup_matrix (size, size);
    init_matrix(a, b, size, size);/* initialize data */
    m_set_procs(3);/* set # of processes */

        /*
         * Include the following line when running DYNIX to flush
         * standard error.  This is done automatically for you
       * under DYNIX/ptx.
       *
         *   fflush(stderr);
         *
         */

    m_fork(matmul,a,b,c, size, size);/* execute matmul */
    m_kill_procs();/* kill child processes */
    print_mats(a, b, c, size, size);/* print results */
}

/* initialize matrix function */

float **setup_matrix(nrows, ncols)
int nrows, ncols;
{
    int i;
    float **new_matrix;

  /*
   * allocate pointer arrays : set new_matrix to
   * address of newly allocated shared matrix
   */

    new_matrix = (float**) shmalloc((unsigned)nrows*(sizeof(float*)));
```

```
    /*
     * allocate data arrays : set first element of
     * new_matrix to address of first element of
     * newly allocated data array
     */

    new_matrix[0] = (float*)shmalloc((unsigned)nrows*ncols*(sizeof(float)));

    /*
     * initialize pointer arrays : set each element of
     * new_matrix to address of corresponding element
     * of data array
     */

    for (i = 1; i < nrows; i++) {
        new_matrix[i] = new_matrix[0] + (ncols * i);
    }
    return (new_matrix);
}

/* initialize matrix function */

void init_matrix(a, b, nrows, ncols)
float **a, **b;
int nrows, ncols;
{
    int i, j;

    for (i = 0; i < nrows; i++) {
        for (j = 0; j < ncols; j++) {
            a[i][j] = (float)i + j;
            b[i][j] = (float)i - j;
        }
    }
}
void matmul(a, b, c, nrows, ncols)
float **a, **b, **c;
int nrows, ncols;
{
    int i, j, k, nprocs;

    nprocs = m_get_numprocs();
    for (i = m_get_myid(); i < nrows; i += nprocs) {
        for (k = 0; k < ncols; k++) {
            c[i][k] = 0.0;
            for (j = 0; j < ncols; j++) {
                c[i][k] += a[i][j] * b[j][k];
```

```
            }
        }
    }
}
void print_mats(a, b, c, nrows, ncols)
float **a, **b, **c;
int nrows, ncols;
{
    int i, j;

    for (i = 0; i < nrows; i++) {
        for (j = 0; j < ncols; j++) {
            printf("\na[%d][%d] = %3.2f\tb[%d][%d] = %3.2f",
                    i, j, a[i][j], i, j, b[i][j]);
            printf("\tc[%d][%d] = %3.2f\n", i, j, c[i][j]);
        }
    }
}
```

A.3 C++ Examples

This section contains three data partitioning examples coded in C++. These examples were compiled with the ptx/C++ compiler and executed on a Symmetry system running DYNIX/ptx 1.2 and on a Symmetry system running DYNIX 3.1.

Static Scheduling

```
/*
 * Multiply two matrices, store results in third matrix,
 * and print results.
 *
 * To compile under DYNIX/ptx: CC -Wc,-seq -o Cstatic cstatic.C -lpps -lseq
 * To compile under DYNIX:     CC -o Cstatic cstatic.C -lpps
 */

#include <sys/types.h>             /* system types header */
#include <stdio.h>                 /* standard I/O header */
#include <parallel/microtask.h>    /* microtasking header */
#include <parallel/parallel.h>     /* parallel library header */

#define SIZE 10                    /* size of matrices */
```

```
/* Global (shared memory) data */

shared_t float a[SIZE][SIZE];        /* first array */
shared_t float b[SIZE][SIZE];        /* second array */
shared_t float c[SIZE][SIZE];        /* result array */

main()
{
    void init_matrix(float [][SIZE], float [][SIZE]);
    void matmul(float [][SIZE], float [][SIZE], float [][SIZE]);
    void print_mats(float [][SIZE], float [][SIZE], float [][SIZE]);
    int nprocs;                      /* number of parallel processes */
    int avail_procs                  /* number of available processors */

    avail_procs = cpus_online();
    fprintf(stderr,"Number of processors available: %d\n",avail_procs);
    fprintf(stderr,"Enter number of processes:");
    scanf("%d",&nprocs);

    init_matrix(a, b);               /* initialize data */
    m_set_procs(nprocs);             /* set # of processes */
    /*
     * Include the next line if running DYNIX to flush
     * standard error.  This is done automatically for you
     * under DYNIX/ptx.
     *
     * fflush(stderr);
     */
    m_fork(matmul, a, b, c);         /* execute parallel loop */
    m_kill_procs();                  /* kill child processes */
    print_mats(a, b, c);             /* print results */
}

/* initialize matrix function */

void init_matrix(float a[][SIZE], float b[][SIZE]);
{
    int i, j;

    for (i = 0; i < SIZE; i++) {
        for (j = 0; j < SIZE; j++) {
            a[i][j] = (float)i + j;
            b[i][j] = (float)i - j;
        }
    }
}
```

```
/* matrix multiply function */

void matmul(float a[][SIZE], float b[][SIZE], float c[][SIZE]);
{
    int i, j, k, nprocs;

    nprocs = m_get_numprocs();          /* no. of processes */
    for (i = m_get_myid(); i < SIZE; i += nprocs) {
        for (j = 0; j < SIZE; j++) {
            for (k = 0; k < SIZE; k++)
                c[i][k] += a[i][j] * b[j][k];
        }
    }
}


/* print results function */

void print_mats(float a[][SIZE], float b[][SIZE], float c[][SIZE]);
{
    int i, j;

    for (i = 0; i < SIZE; i++) {
        for (j = 0; j < SIZE; j++) {
            printf("\na[%d][%d] = %3.2f\tb[%d][%d] = %3.2f",
                i, j, a[i][j], i, j, b[i][j]);
            printf("\tc[%d][%d] = %3.2f\n", i, j, c[i][j]);
        }
    }
}
```

Dynamic Scheduling

```
/*
 * Use Cartesian coordinates to find the city closest to
 * Beaverton, Oregon, and print the name and distance
 * from Beaverton.
 *
 * To compile under DYNIX/ptx: CC -Wc,-seq -o Cdynamic cdynamic.C -lpps
 *           -lm -lseq
 * To compile under DYNIX:     CC -o Cdynamic cdynamic.C -lpps -lm
 */

#include <sys/types.h>              /* system types header */
#include <stdio.h>                  /* standard I/O header */
#include <math.h>                   /* math library header */
```

```
#include <parallel/microtask.h>      /* microtasking header */
#include <parallel/parallel.h>       /* parallel library header */

#define NCITIES 10                   /* number of cities */
#define BITE 1                       /* bite of work */

/* Global shared memory data */

shared_t float shortest;             /* distance to nearest city */
shared_t int closest;                /* index of nearest city */

struct location {
    char *name;
    float x, y;
};

shared_t struct location cities[NCITIES] = {
    { "CHICAGO", 2000., 100. },
    { "DENVER", 500., -550. },
    { "NEW YORK", 150., 100. },
    { "SEATTLE", 0., 200. },
    { "MIAMI", 3500., -2000. },
    { "SAN FRANCISCO", -100., -1000. },
    { "RENO", 200., -600. },
    { "PORTLAND", -17., 0.  },
    { "WASHINGTON D.C.", 3000., -400. },
    { "TILLAMOOK", -70., -50. },
};

shared_t struct location beaverton = { "BEAVERTON", 0., 0. };

main()
{
    void find_dis(struct location*);

    shortest = 999999999.;
    m_fork(find_dis, cities);
    printf("%s is closest to Beaverton.\n",
      cities[closest].name);
    printf("%s is %3.2f miles from Beaverton.\n",
      cities[closest].name, shortest);
}
```

```
/* find distance to nearest city */

void find_dis(struct location* cities)
{
    int i, base, top;   /* local loop index, start & end value */
    float xsqdis, ysqdis, dist;

    while ((base = BITE*(m_next( )-1)) < NCITIES) {
    top = base + BITE;                  /* take a bite of work */
    if (top >= NCITIES) top = NCITIES-1;

        /* execute all iterations in bite of work */

        for (i = base; i < top; i++) {
            xsqdis = pow(fabs(beaverton.x - cities[i].x),2.);
            ysqdis = pow(fabs(beaverton.y - cities[i].y),2.);
            dist   = sqrt(xsqdis + ysqdis);
            m_lock();
            if (dist < shortest) {
                closest = i;
                shortest = dist;
            }
            m_unlock();
        }
    }
}
```

Dynamic Shared Memory Allocation

```
/*
 * Multiply two matrices, store results in third
 * matrix, and print results.
 *
 * To compile under DYNIX/ptx: CC -Wc,-seq -o Shmem shmem.C shnew.o
 *          -lpps -lseq
 * To compile under DYNIX:     CC -o Shmem shmem.C shnew.o -lpps
 */

#include <sys/types.h>           /* system types header */
#include <stdio.h>               /* standard I/O header */
#include <parallel/microtask.h>  /* microtasking header */
#include <parallel/parallel.h>   /* parallel library header */
```

```
/* Global shared memory data */

shared_t float **a;                 /* first array */
shared_t float **b;                 /* second array */
shared_t float **c;                 /* result array */

main()
{
    float **setup_matrix(int, int);
    void init_matrix(float**, float**, int, int);
    void matmul(float**, float**, float**, int, int);
    void print_mats(float**, float**, float**, int, int);
    int size ;                      /* loop end value and loop increment */

    fprintf(stderr,"Enter array size:");
    scanf("%d",&size);

    a = setup_matrix (size, size);  /* allocate shared */
    b = setup_matrix (size, size);  /*     memory      */
    c = setup_matrix (size, size);
    init_matrix(a, b, size, size);  /* initialize data */

/*
 * Include the next line if running DYNIX to flush
 * standard error.  This is done automatically for you
 * under DYNIX/ptx.
 *
 *  fflush(stderr);
 */
    m_set_procs(3);                 /* set # of processes */
    m_fork(matmul,a,b,c,size,size); /* execute matmul */
    m_kill_procs();                 /* kill child processes */
    print_mats(a, b, c, size, size); /* print results */
}

/* initialize matrix function */

float **setup_matrix(int nrows, int ncols)
{
    int i;
    float **new_matrix;
```

```
/*
 * allocate pointer arrays : set new_matrix to
 * address of newly allocated shared matrix
 */

  new_matrix = new float*[nrows];

/*
 * allocate data arrays : set first element of
 * new_matrix to address of first element of
 * newly allocated data array
 */

  new_matrix[0] = new float[nrows*ncols];

/*
 * initialize pointer arrays : set each element of
 * new_matrix to address of corresponding element
 * of data array
 */

  for (i = 1; i < nrows; i++) {
      new_matrix[i] = new_matrix[0] + (ncols * i);
  }
  return (new_matrix);
}

/* initialize matrix function */

void init_matrix(float **a, float **b, int nrows, int ncols)
{
    int i, j;

    for (i = 0; i < nrows; i++) {
        for (j = 0; j < ncols; j++) {
            a[i][j] = (float)i + j;
            b[i][j] = (float)i - j;
        }
    }
}
```

```
void matmul(float **a, float **b, float **c, int nrows, int ncols)
{
    int i, j, k, nprocs;

    nprocs = m_get_numprocs();
    for (i = m_get_myid(); i < nrows; i += nprocs) {
        for (k = 0; k < ncols; k++) {
            c[i][k] = 0.0;
            for (j = 0; j < ncols; j++) {
                c[i][k] += a[i][j] * b[j][k];
            }
        }
    }
}

void print_mats(float **a, float **b, float **c, int nrows, int ncols)
{
    int i, j;

    for (i = 0; i < nrows; i++) {
        for (j = 0; j < ncols; j++) {
            printf("\na[%d][%d] = %3.2f\tb[%d][%d] = %3.2f",
                i, j, a[i][j], i, j, b[i][j]);
            printf("\tc[%d][%d] = %3.2f\n", i, j, c[i][j]);
        }
    }
}
```

The following is a listing for *shnew.C*, which must be linked with the program:

```
// To compile under DYNIX/ptx: CC -Wc,-seq -c shnew.C
// To compile under DYNIX:      CC -c shnew.C
//
#include <stddef.h>

extern "C" char* shmalloc(unsigned);

void* operator new(size_t size)
{
    return (void*) shmalloc(unsigned(size));
}
```

A.4 FORTRAN Examples

This section contains three data partitioning examples coded in FORTRAN. These examples were compiled with the ptx/FORTRAN compiler and on a Symmetry system running DYNIX/ptx 1.2 and on a Symmetry system running DYNIX.

```
C
C Perform a matrix multiply for a square matrix
C (number of rows = number of columns)
C
C To compile: fortran -mp -o matmul matmul.f
C
      PROGRAM MATRIX_MULTIPLY
C
      PARAMETER (NROWS = 10, NCOLS = 10)
      REAL R(NROWS, NCOLS), S(NROWS,NCOLS), T(NROWS,NCOLS)
      INTEGER N
C
      N = NROWS


C
C Perform the necessary setup.
C
      CALL SETUP(R, S, T, NROWS, NCOLS)
C
C Perform the matrix multiply.
C
      CALL MATMUL(R, S, T, NROWS, NCOLS)
C
C Print the result.
C
      DO 20 I=1,N
      DO 20 J=1,N
         WRITE(6,10) I, J, R(I,J)
 10      FORMAT('I = ', I2, 3X, 'J = ', I2, 3X, 'R(I,J)= ', F8.2)
 20   CONTINUE
      END
C
C
C
```

```
      SUBROUTINE SETUP(A, B, C, NROWS, NCOLS)
C
      INTEGER N
      REAL A(NROWS,NCOLS), B(NROWS,NCOLS), C(NROWS,NCOLS)
C
      N = NROWS
C
      DO 10 I=1,N
      DO 10 J=1,N
         A(I,J) = 0.0
         B(I,J) = FLOAT(I+J)
         C(I,J) = FLOAT(I-J)
  10  CONTINUE
C
      RETURN
      END
C
C
C
      SUBROUTINE MATMUL(A, B, C, NROWS, NCOLS)
C
      REAL A(NROWS,NCOLS), B(NROWS,NCOLS), C(NROWS,NCOLS)
      INTEGER N
C
      N = NROWS
C
C$DOACROSS SHARE(A, B, C, N), LOCAL(K,J)
      DO 10 I = 1, N
      DO 10 K = 1, N
      DO 10 J = 1, N
         A(I,J) = A(I,J) + B(I,J) * C(K,J)
  10  CONTINUE
C
      RETURN
      END
```

```
C
C Use Cartesian coordinates to find the city closes to
C Beaverton, Oregon, and print the name of that city and its
C distance from Beaverton.
C
C To compile: fortran -mp -o find_distance find_distance.f
C
      PROGRAM FIND_DISTANCE
C
C Declare variables.
C
      INTEGER X, Y, N, I, CLOSEST, NCITIES
      CHARACTER*15 CITY_NAMES(10)
      REAL BVRTN(2), COORDINATES(10,10)
      REAL LEAST, DIST
C
C Initialize data.
C
      BVRTN(1) = 0.
      BVRTN(2) = 0.
      CITY_NAMES(1) = "Chicago"
      CITY_NAMES(2) = "Denver"
      CITY_NAMES(3) = "New York"
      CITY_NAMES(4) = "Seattle"
      CITY_NAMES(5) = "Miami"
      CITY_NAMES(6) = "San Francisco"
      CITY_NAMES(7) = "Reno"
      CITY_NAMES(8) = "Portland"
      CITY_NAMES(9) = "Washington D.C."
      CITY_NAMES(10) = "Tillamook"
C
      COORDINATES(1,1) = 2000.
      COORDINATES(1,2) = 100.
      COORDINATES(2,1) = 500.
      COORDINATES(2,2) = -550.
      COORDINATES(3,1) = 150.
      COORDINATES(3,2) = 100.
      COORDINATES(4,1) = 0.
      COORDINATES(4,2) = 200.
      COORDINATES(5,1) = 3500.
      COORDINATES(5,2) = -2000.
      COORDINATES(6,1) = -100.
```

```
      COORDINATES(6,2) = -1000.
      COORDINATES(7,1) = 200.
      COORDINATES(7,2) = -600.
      COORDINATES(8,1) = -17.
      COORDINATES(8,2) = 0.
      COORDINATES(9,1) = 3000.
      COORDINATES(9,2) = -400.
      COORDINATES(10,1) = -70.
      COORDINATES(10,2) = -50.

C
      NCITIES = 10
      X = 1
      Y = 2
      LEAST = 9999999.0
C
C Now find the distance.
C
C$DOACROSS SHARE(BVRTN, COORDINATES, CLOSEST, LEAST, X, Y),
C$&                 LOCAL(XSQDIS, YSQDIS, DIST), LOCKS(iguard)
      DO 10 I = 1, NCITIES
          XSQDIS = (BVRTN(X)-COORDINATES(I,X))**2
          YSQDIS = (BVRTN(Y)-COORDINATES(I,Y))**2
          DIST = SQRT(XSQDIS + YSQDIS)
C$LOCK iguard
          IF (DIST.LT.LEAST) THEN
              CLOSEST = I
              LEAST = DIST
          ENDIF
C$UNLOCK iguard
  10  CONTINUE
C
C Print the result.
C
      WRITE(6,20) CITY_NAMES(CLOSEST)
      WRITE(6,30) CITY_NAMES(CLOSEST), LEAST
  20  FORMAT(A8,1X, 'is closest to Beaverton.')
  30  FORMAT(A8,1X, 'is', F6.2, ' miles from Beaverton.')
C
      END
```

A.5 Pascal Examples

This section contains three data partitioning examples coded in Pascal. These examples were compiled with the ptx/PASCAL compiler and executed on a Symmetry system running DYNIX/ptx and on a Symmetry system running DYNIX.

Static Scheduling

```
{ multiply two matrices, store results in third
          matrix, and print results

  to compile: pce -mp -o pstatic pstatic.p
}

program matrix_mul(input,output) ;

import ParallelMicrotasking;

const
SIZE = 9 ;                          { (size of matrices)-1 }

type
matrix = array[0..SIZE, 0..SIZE] of real;
integer = longinteger;

var
a : matrix ;                        { first array }
b : matrix ;                        { second array }
c : matrix ;                        { result array }

nprocs: longinteger; { number of processes }

ret_val: longinteger; { return value for m_set_procs }
```

```
{ initialize matrix function }

procedure init_matrix ;

var
i, j : integer ;

begin
    for i := 0 to SIZE do
    begin
        for j := 0 to SIZE do
        begin
            a[i, j] := (i + j) ;
            b[i, j] := (i - j) ;
        end;
    end;
end; { init_matrix }

{ matrix multiply function }

procedure matmul ;

var
i, j, k : integer;{ local loop indices }
nprocs  : integer;{ number of processes }

begin
    nprocs := m_get_numprocs;{ number of processes }
    i := m_get_myid;{ start at Nth iteration }
    while (i <= SIZE) do
    begin
        for j := 0 to SIZE do
        begin
            for k := 0 to SIZE do
            c[i, k] := c[i, k] + a[i, j] * b[j, k];
        end;
        i := i + nprocs;
    end;
end; { matmul}
```

```
{ print results procedure }

procedure print_mats ;

var
i, j : integer;{ local loop indices }

begin
    for i := 0 to SIZE do
    begin
        for j := 0 to SIZE do
        begin

            writeln('a[',i :1,',',j :1,'] = ',a[i,j] :6:2, ' ',
                'b[',i :1,',',j :1,'] = ',b[i,j] :6:2, ' ',
                'c[',i :1,',',j :1,'] = ',c[i,j] :6:2)
        end;
    end;
end; {print_mats}

begin { main program starts here}

    writeln('Enter number of processes:');
    readln(nprocs);
    init_matrix;                        { initialize data arrays }

    ret_val := m_set_procs(nprocs);     { set number of processes }
    ret_val := p_fork(matmul);          { do matrix multiply }
    m_kill_procs;                       { terminate child processes }
    print_mats;                         { print results }

end. { main program }
```

Dynamic Scheduling

```
{ Use Cartesian coordinates to find the city closest
   to Beaverton, Oregon, and print the name and
   distance from Beaverton.

  To compile: pascal -mp -o pdynamic pdynamic.p
}

program find_distance(input,output) ;

import ParallelMicrotasking;

const
NCITIES = 10;                       { number of cities }
BITE = 1;                           { bite of work }

type
cityrecord =
    record
     name : string (15);            { names of cities }
     x : real;                      { x coordinates }
     y : real                       { y coordinates }
    end;

var
closest : integer ;                 { index of nearest city }
shortest : real ;                   {distance to nearest city }
cities : array[1..NCITIES] of cityrecord ;{ city info }
beaverton : cityrecord ;            { coordinates of Beaverton }
ret_value : longinteger;


{ initialize array of city data }

procedure init_cities ;

begin

    cities[1].name := 'CHICAGO';
    cities[1].x := 2000.0;
    cities[1].y := 100.0;
    cities[2].name := 'DENVER';
    cities[2].x := 500.0;
    cities[2].y := -550.0;
    cities[3].name := 'NEW YORK';
    cities[3].x := 1500.0;
```

```
    cities[3].y := 100.0;
    cities[4].name := 'SEATTLE';
    cities[4].x := 0.0;
    cities[4].y := 200.0;
    cities[5].name := 'MIAMI';
    cities[5].x := 3500.0;
    cities[5].y := 2000.0;
    cities[6].name := 'SAN FRANCISCO';
    cities[6].x := -100.0;
    cities[6].y := -1000.0;
    cities[7].name := 'RENO';
    cities[7].x := 200.0;
    cities[7].y := -600.0;
    cities[8].name := 'PORTLAND';
    cities[8].x := -17.0;
    cities[8].y := 0.0;
    cities[9].name := 'WASHINGTON D.C';
    cities[9].x := 3000.0;
    cities[9].y := -400.0;
    cities[10].name := 'TILLAMOOK';
    cities[10].x := -70.0;
    cities[10].y := -50.0;

    beaverton.name := 'BEAVERTON';
    beaverton.x := 0.0;
    beaverton.y := 0.0;

end; { of init_cities }


{ find distance to nearest city }

procedure find_dis;

var
i, base, top : longinteger ;              { local index, start value, end value }
xsqdis, ysqdis, dist : real ;

begin
    base := BITE * m_next;
    while (base < NCITIES) do
    begin
        top := base + BITE;
        i := base;
        while (i < top) do
        begin
            xsqdis := sqr(beaverton.x - cities[i].x);
```

```
                 ysqdis := sqr(beaverton.y - cities[i].y);
                 dist   := sqrt(xsqdis + ysqdis);

                 m_lock;
                 if (dist < shortest) then
                 begin
                 closest := i;
                 shortest := dist;
                 end;
                 m_unlock;

                 i := i + 1 ;
             end;
         base := BITE * m_next;
         end;
end;

begin { main program starts here }

    shortest := 999999999.0;

    init_cities;
    ret_value := p_fork(find_dis);
    writeln(cities[closest].name,
        ' is closest to Beaverton.');
    writeln(cities[closest].name, ' is ', shortest:4:2,
        ' miles from Beaverton.');

end.
```

Appendix B
Parallel-Programming Library

This appendix contains the DYNIX/ptx man pages for the parallel-programming library routines. These man pages are included to give you a better idea of the capabilities and use of the parallel-programming library. However, the man pages in the *DYNIX/ptx Reference Manual* may contain more up-to-date information.

NAME

intro – introduction to the parallel-programming library

DESCRIPTION

These routines compose the parallel-programming library, which supports microtasking and multitasking in C, C++, Pascal, and FORTRAN programs. (For information on microtasking and multitasking programming models, refer to the *Guide to Parallel Programming*.)

The routines are contained in the file */usr/lib/libpps.a*. These routines are linked into a program by including the **–lpps** and **–lseq** options in the **cc**, **CC**, or **ld** command line, or by using the **–mp** option in the **fortran** or **pascal** command line.

For an overview of how the parallel-programming library routines are used, and for sample programs and related information, refer to the *Guide to Parallel Programming*.

Environment Variables

PARALLEL   Specifies the number of processes to execute in parallel. You can use the **getenv**() C library function to find out the current value of the **PARALLEL** environment variable from your program.

TMPPATH   Some of these routines allocate file space in the directory specified by the **TMPPATH** environment variable. If **TMPPATH** is not defined, routines allocate file system space from the following directories in the order listed below:

1. current directory
2. directory specified by the **HOME** environment variable
3. */usr/tmp*
4. */tmp*

LIST OF FUNCTIONS

The following routines support microtasking:

Name	Appears on Page	Description
m_fork	m_fork.3pps	execute a subprogram in parallel
m_get_myid	m_get_myid.3pps	return process identification
m_get_numprocs	m_get_numprocs.3pps	get number of child processes
m_kill_procs	m_kill_procs.3pps	kill child processes
m_lock	m_lock.3pps	initialize and lock a lock
m_next	m_next.3pps	increment global counter
m_park_procs	m_park_procs.3pps	suspend child process execution
m_rele_procs	m_park_procs.3pps	resume child process execution
m_set_procs	m_set_procs.3pps	set number of child processes
m_sync	m_sync.3pps	check in at barrier
m_unlock	m_lock.3pps	unlock a lock

The following routines support multitasking:

Name	Appears on Page	Description
cpus_online	cpus_online.3pps	return number of CPUs online
s_clock	s_lock.3pps	lock a lock, return if unsuccessful
S_CLOCK	s_lock.3pps	lock a lock, return if unsuccessful (C macro)
s_init_barrier	s_wait_barrier.3pps	initialize a barrier
S_INIT_BARRIER	s_wait_barrier.3pps	initialize a barrier (C macro)
s_init_lock	s_lock.3pps	initialize a lock
S_INIT_LOCK	s_lock.3pps	initialize a lock (C macro)
s_lock	s_lock.3pps	lock a lock
S_LOCK	s_lock.3pps	lock a lock (C macro)
s_unlock	s_lock.3pps	unlock a lock
S_UNLOCK	s_lock.3pps	unlock a lock (C macro)
s_wait_barrier	s_wait_barrier.3pps	wait at a barrier
S_WAIT_BARRIER	s_wait_barrier.3pps	wait at a barrier (C macro)

The following routines support memory allocation for parallel programming. The **brk** and **sbrk** routines are available without loading the parallel-programming library (see **brk**(2)), but the versions in the parallel-programming library are necessary for compatibility with the rest of the library.

Name	Appears on Page	Description
brk	brk.3pps	change private data segment size
sbrk	brk.3pps	change private data segment size
shbrk	shbrk.3pps	change shared data segment size
shfree	shmalloc.3pps	deallocate shared data memory
shmalloc	shmalloc.3pps	allocate shared data memory
shrealloc	shmalloc.3pps	reallocate shared data memory
shsbrk	shbrk.3pps	change shared data segment size

NOTES

The **SYNOPSIS** section of each man pages lists any required include files and the definition of a routine, not the declaration or call itself.

The **m_single**() and **m_multi**() routines are no longer supported. Sequent recommends you replace calls to these routines with calls to **msync**() and **m_get_myid**() as indicated below:

Before	After
m_single();	m_sync(); if (m_get_myid() == 0) {
...	...
	}
m_multi();	m_sync();

NAME

brk, sbrk – change private data segment size

SYNOPSIS

C syntax:

#include <parallel/parallel.h>
caddr_t brk(addr)
caddr_t addr;

caddr_t sbrk(incr)
int incr;

C++ syntax

#include <parallel/parallel.h>
extern "C" caddr brk(caddr_t addr)

extern "C" caddr sbrk(int incr)

Pascal syntax

FORTRAN syntax

DESCRIPTION

These routines are identical to the standard **brk** and **sbrk** (see **brk(2)**) routines except that these routines verify that the private data segment does not overlap the shared data segment which follows it. If the **brk** or **sbrk** call will cause the segments to overlap, the routine issues an error.

ERRORS

If an error occurs, the return value is –1 and the variable **errno** contains the error code associated with one of the following:

[ENOMEM]   The requested private data segment will overlap the shared data segment.

[ENOMEM]   The routine cannot allocate file system space to expand the file which has been memory mapped to the shared data segment (see **mmap**(2SEQ)). The routine tries to allocate file system space from directories in the following order:

1. directory indicated by **TMPPATH** environment variable
2. current directory
3. user's home directory
4. directory */usr/tmp*
5. directory */tmp*

SEE ALSO

execve(2), malloc(3), end(3), vm_ctl(2SEQ)

NOTES

The gap between the private data segment and the shared data segment can be adjusted by passing language directives to the linker. For example, the following *ifile* changes the separation between the end of .bss and the beginning of .shdata from 0x80000 (default) to 0x100000 (1 megabyte):

```
/* Note: the value 0x100000 used in this file can be changed to specify
 * more or less space, but it must always be a multiple of 0x1000.
 */
SECTIONS
{
        /* Leave enough room for headers before starting .text */
        .text 0x200 BLOCK(0x200) : { *(.init) *(.text) }

        /* .data and .bss are just like the default */
        GROUP BIND (NEXT(0x1000) + ((SIZEOF(.text) + ADDR(.text)) % 0x1000)) :
        {
                .data      : { }
                .bss       : { }
        }

        /* All this just to say 0x100000 (1 MB) beyond the end .bss,
         * then align to the next page.
         */
        GROUP BIND
          ( 0x100000  /* <-- Adjust this to change .bss to .shdata gap */

          /* end of .bss */
          + NEXT(0x1000) + ( ( SIZEOF(.text) + ADDR(.text) ) % 0x1000 )
          + SIZEOF(.data) + SIZEOF(.bss)

          /* align to next page */
          + 0x1000
          - ( ( ( ( SIZEOF(.text) + ADDR(.text) ) % 0x1000 )
               + SIZEOF(.data) + SIZEOF(.bss) ) % 0x1000 )
          ) BLOCK (0x1000) :
        {
                .shdata   : { }
                .shbss  : { }
        }

        /* Like the default */
        .comment BLOCK(0x1000) : { *(.comment) }
}
```

Now use the following command to link the directives in *ifile*:

cc –Wc,–seq –o foo foo.c –lpps –lseq ifile

Refer to the linker documentation in the *DYNIX/ptx C and Language Tools* binder for more information about ifiles.

When **brk** and **sbrk** increase a program's address space, they also attempt to increase its allowable resident set size (see **vm_ctl**(2SEQ)).

NAME

cpus_online – returns the number of CPUs online

SYNOPSIS

C syntax

int cpus_online ()

C++ syntax

#include <parallel/parallel.h>
extern "C" int cpus_online()

Pascal syntax

import ParallelMultitasking;
          or
function cpus_online : integer; external;

FORTRAN syntax

integer*4 function cpus_online

DESCRIPTION

The **cpus_online** routine returns the number of processors currently configured and online.

SEE ALSO

tmp_ctl(2SEQ), *Guide to Parallel Programming*

NAME

m_fork, p_fork – execute a subprogram in parallel

SYNOPSIS

C syntax:

#include <parallel/microtask.h>
int m_fork(func[,arg,...])
void (*func)();
sometype args;

C++ syntax:

#include <parallel/microtask.h>
extern "C" int m_fork(func[,arg,...])
void (*func)();
sometype args;

Pascal syntax

import ParallelMicrotasking;
            or
function p_fork(procedure func) : integer; external;
procedure func(arg: sometype;...);
i=p_fork(func[,arg,...]);

FORTRAN syntax

external func
integer*4 m_fork
i=m_fork(func[,arg,...])

DESCRIPTION

The **m_fork** or **p_fork** (Pascal only) routines assign a subprogram to child
processes, which then cooperate in executing the subprogram in parallel.
(Note that the parent process also executes the subprogram in parallel with
the child processes.) The number of child processes used by the **m_fork** call
can be set with a previous call to **m_set_procs**. If **m_set_procs** has not been
called, the number of child processes defaults to *(number of CPUs online) /2*.
If the program has no child processes from previous **m_fork** calls, the call creates the child processes. If there are already child processes from a previous
call, **m_fork** reuses the existing processes.

When an **m_fork** call creates child processes, each child process is given a private integer variable called *m_myid*, which identifies it within the set of child
processes being created. The first child process's identification number is 1,
the second's is 2, and so on. You can call the routine **m_get_myid** to find out
the identification number of a child process (see **m_get_myid**(3PPS)).

For C programs, the header file */usr/include/parallel/microtask.h* contains
an external declaration of the variable *m_myid* and the variable *m_numprocs*,
which indicates the total number of processes executing the subprogram
(including all the child processes and the parent process).

Once child processes are available, **m_fork** starts them executing the subprogram **func** with the given arguments. For Pascal programs, **func** cannot be
nested — it must be declared at the outermost level of a procedure or module
block. The child processes execute the subprogram until they all return from

it. At this point, the program returns from the **m_fork** call and the child processes spin, waiting for more work. The program can either kill the child processes with a call to the routine **m_kill**, suspend them with a call to **m_park_procs**, or let the child processes spin until they are reused by another **m_fork** call. If the child processes are to be reused, the **m_park_procs** offers the most efficient use of the Sequent system, because it saves the CPU usage of having the processes spin and it saves the overhead of having to recreate processes on the next **m_fork** call.

You must ensure that arguments passed to the subprogram **func** are either call-by-value arguments or addresses of data in shared memory. They must not be addresses in the parent's private data segment.

ERRORS

The **m_fork** call fails and no child processes are created if any of the following error conditions occurs:

[EAGAIN]   The **m_fork** call would exceed *NPROC*, the system's limit on the total number of executing processes.

[EINVAL]   This call to **m_fork** is nested within a previous call.

NOTES

Each call to **m_fork** resets the global counter (see **m_next**(3PPS)).

It is the user's responsibility to provide a priority mechanism to schedule parallel programs. Performance significantly degrades whenever the number of system processes exceeds the number of processors since programs may be waiting for a process that has been preempted.

SEE ALSO

shmalloc(3PPS), brk(3PPS), m_set_procs(3PPS), m_kill_procs(3PPS), m_next(3PPS), *Guide to Parallel Programming*

NAME

m_get_myid – return process identification

SYNOPSIS

C syntax:

#include <parallel/microtask.h>
int m_get_myid()

C++ syntax:

#include <parallel/microtask.h>
extern "C" int m_get_myid()

Pascal syntax

import ParallelMicrotasking;

or

function m_get_myid : integer; external;

FORTRAN syntax

integer*4 function m_get_myid

DESCRIPTION

The **m_get_myid** routine returns the value of the variable **m_myid**, the process's identification number. For the parent process, this variable has the value zero. Child processes are assigned identification numbers in the order of their creation: the first child process has identification number 1, the second has 2, and so on. The C header file */usr/include/parallel/microtask.h* contains an external declaration of the variable **m_myid**.

SEE ALSO

m_fork(3PPS), *Guide to Parallel Programming*

NAME

> m_get_numprocs – return number of child processes

SYNOPSIS

> *C syntax:*

> **#include <parallel/microtask.h>**
> **int m_get_numprocs()**

> *C++ syntax:*

> **#include <parallel/microtask.h>**
> **extern "C" int m_get_numprocs()**

> *Pascal syntax*

> **import ParallelMicrotasking;**
>   *or*
> **function m_get_numprocs : integer; external;**

> *FORTRAN syntax*

> **integer*4 function m_get_numprocs**

DESCRIPTION

> The **m_get_numprocs** routine returns the value of the variable
> **m_numprocs**, the current number of processes in the program. This value
> reflects the number of child processes plus one, the parent process. The C
> header file */usr/include/parallel/microtask.h* contains an external declara-
> tion of the variable **m_numprocs**.

SEE ALSO

> m_set_procs(3PPS), *Guide to Parallel Programming*

NAME

m_kill_procs – kill child processes

SYNOPSIS

C syntax:

#include <parallel/microtask.h>
int m_kill_procs()

C++ syntax:

#include <parallel/microtask.h>
extern "C" int m_kill_procs()

Pascal syntax

import ParallelMicrotasking;
       or
procedure m_kill_procs ; external;

FORTRAN syntax

subroutine m_kill_procs

DESCRIPTION

The **m_kill_procs** routine terminates the child processes created by a previous call to **m_fork**.

The **m_kill_procs** routine fails if it is called from a subprogram invoked by an **m_fork** call.

If no errors occur, the return value is 0.

ERRORS

If the following error condition occurs, the return value is set to –1 and the variable **errno** contains the associated error code:

[EINVAL]   Some child processes are still executing within an **m_fork** call.

SEE ALSO

m_fork(3PPS), *Guide to Parallel Programming*

NAME

m_lock, m_unlock – lock, unlock locks

SYNOPSIS

C syntax:

#include <parallel/microtask.h>
m_lock()
m_unlock()

C++ syntax:

#include <parallel/microtask.h>
extern "C" m_lock()
extern "C" m_unlock()

Pascal syntax

import ParallelMicrotasking;
                    or
procedure m_lock; external;
procedure m_unlock; external;

FORTRAN syntax

subroutine m_lock
subroutine m_unlock

DESCRIPTION

The **m_lock** and **m_unlock** routines are microtasking interfaces to a single
slock_t-type lock. For a single lock, they are easier to use than the
s_init_lock, **s_lock**, and **s_unlock** routines because they don't require you to
declare or initialize the lock before using it. They are also faster than the
other routines because they do not pass the lock address as an argument.

m_lock locks the lock. **m_lock** is always successful; it spins as long as is necessary to acquire the lock.

m_unlock unlocks the lock.

SEE ALSO

intro(3PPS), s_lock(3PPS), shmalloc(3PPS), *Guide to Parallel Programming*

NAME

m_next – increment global counter

SYNOPSIS

C syntax:

#include <parallel/microtask.h>
int m_next()

C++ syntax:

#include <parallel/microtask.h>
extern "C" int m_next()

Pascal syntax

import ParallelMicrotasking;
       or
function m_next : integer; external;

FORTRAN syntax

integer*4 function m_next

DESCRIPTION

The **m_next** routine atomically increments a global counter. The program's first call to **m_next** returns the value 1, the second returns 2, and so on. Calls to the **m_fork** or **m_sync** routines reset the global counter to zero.

SEE ALSO

m_fork(3PPS), m_sync(3PPS), *Guide to Parallel Programming*

NAME

m_park_procs, m_rele_procs – suspend and resume child process execution

SYNOPSIS

C syntax:

#include <parallel/microtask.h>
int m_park_procs()
int m_rele_procs()

C++ syntax:

#include <parallel/microtask.h>
extern "C" int m_park_procs()
extern "C" int m_rele_procs()

Pascal syntax

import ParallelMicrotasking;
                     or
procedure m_park_procs; external;
procedure m_rele_procs; external;

FORTRAN syntax

subroutine m_park_procs
subroutine m_rele_procs

DESCRIPTION

The **m_park_procs** routine suspends execution of child processes created by
an **m_fork** call. Typically, you would suspend child processes while the parent process is doing extensive I/O or setting up another phase of the program.
The **m_rele_procs** routine resumes child process execution when the child
processes are again required.

Do not call **m_park_procs** when **m_fork** is executing. Likewise, do not call
m_park_procs when the child processes are already suspended.

If no errors occur, the return value is 0.

ERRORS

If the following error condition occurs, the return value is set to –1 and the
variable **errno** contains the associated error code:

[EINVAL]   The routine was called in an inappropriate context. For
              example, the routine was called from a subprogram executing
              in an **m_fork** call, or the processes were already suspended.

SEE ALSO

Guide to Parallel Programming

NAME

m_set_procs – set number of child processes

SYNOPSIS

C syntax:

#include <parallel/microtask.h>
int m_set_procs(nprocs)
int nprocs;

C++ syntax:

#include <parallel/microtask.h>
extern "C" int m_set_procs(int nprocs)

Pascal syntax

import ParallelMicrotasking;
            or
function m_set_procs (nprocs : integer) : integer; external;

FORTRAN syntax

integer*4 function m_set_procs(nprocs)
integer*4 nprocs

DESCRIPTION

The **m_set_procs** routine declares the number of processes to execute subprograms in parallel on subsequent calls to **m_fork**. The argument **nprocs** declares the total number of processes that will run in parallel, including the parent process and the child processes. If **nprocs** is zero, the program creates no child processes, but all barriers and locks are initialized as if the program were going to create child processes.

The **m_set_procs** routine initializes a shared variable called **m_numprocs**, which controls the number of processes created by subsequent calls to **m_fork**. The C header file */usr/include/parallel/microtask.h* contains an external declaration of **m_numprocs**, as well as the constant MAXPROCS which determines the maximum number of processes that the system will allow the program to create. The other limiting factor is the number of CPUs online: **nprocs** can be no more than the number of CPUs online minus one.

The **m_set_procs** routine is optional: if the program does not call this routine before calling **m_fork**, the number of processes defaults to *(number of CPUs online)/2*. The program must not call **m_set_procs** while the child processes from an **m_fork** call are still alive (that is, before an **m_kill_procs** call to kill the child processes).

ERRORS

If an **m_set_procs** call is successful, the return value is zero. If one of the following error conditions occur, the return value is set to –1 and the variable **errno** contains the associated error code:

[EINVAL]   The argument **nprocs** is greater than MAXPROCS or it is greater than or equal to the number of online CPUs.

[EINVAL]   Children from an **m_fork** call are already running. In this case, call **m_kill_procs** to kill the existing child processes before calling **m_set_procs**.

SEE ALSO

m_fork(3PPS), m_kill_procs(3PPS), *Guide to Parallel Programming*

NAME

      m_sync – check in at barrier

SYNOPSIS

      C syntax:

      #include <parallel/microtask.h>
      void m_sync()

      C++ syntax:

      #include <parallel/microtask.h>
      extern "C" m_sync()

      Pascal syntax

      import ParallelMicrotasking;
                  or
      procedure m_sync; external;

      FORTRAN syntax

      subroutine m_sync

DESCRIPTION

      The **m_sync** routine causes a process to spin until all cooperating processes
      have reached the same point and called **m_sync**. The program must not call
      the **m_sync** routine unless there are multiple processes executing; that is,
      unless the program is executing a subprogram during an **m_fork** call and is
      not between a pair of **m_lock/m_unlock** or **s_lock/s_unlock** calls.

NOTES

      Calls to **m_sync** reset the global counter (see **m_next**(3PPS)).

ERRORS

      This routine fails if the following occurs:

      [EINVAL]   There are no child processes executing.

SEE ALSO

      m_set_procs(3PPS), m_fork(3PPS), m_park_procs(3PPS), m_kill_procs(3PPS),
      m_next(3PPS) , *Guide to Parallel Programming*

NAME

s_init_lock, s_lock, s_clock, s_unlock – initialize, lock, unlock locks

SYNOPSIS

C syntax:

#include <parallel/parallel.h>
slock_t magiclock, *lp = &magiclock;
s_init_lock (lp)
S_INIT_LOCK (lp)
s_lock (lp)
S_LOCK (lp)
s_clock (lp)
S_CLOCK (lp)
s_unlock (lp)
S_UNLOCK (lp)

C++ syntax:

#include <parallel/parallel.h>
extern "C" s_init_lock(slock_t *lp)
extern "C" s_lock(slock_t *lp)
extern "C" int s_clock(slock_t *lp)
extern "C" s_unlock(slock_t *lp)

Pascal syntax

import ParallelMultitasking;
                or
procedure s_init_lock(var lp : slock_t); external;
procedure s_lock(var lp : slock_t); external;
function s_clock (var lp: slock_t) : boolean; external;
procedure s_unlock(var lp : slock_t); external;

FORTRAN syntax

subroutine s_init_lock(lp)
subroutine s_lock(lp)
subroutine s_clock(lp)
subroutine s_unlock(lp)
integer*1 lp

DESCRIPTION

s_init_lock initializes a memory-based lock. After the lock is initialized, it can be locked with the **s_lock** or **s_clock** routine and unlocked with the **s_unlock** routine. There is no practical limit to the number of locks that can be used by a process.

In C and C++, a lock is a shared data structure of type slock_t, as shown in the following declaration statement:

```
shared slock_t lock; /* "shared_t slock_t lock;" in C++ */
```

In Pascal, a lock is a global integer variable. In FORTRAN, a lock is an INTEGER*1 variable. For both Pascal and FORTRAN routines, a lock is mapped into shared memory when the **–mp** compiler option is specified.

s_lock and **s_clock** lock the lock whose address is **lp**. The lock must previously have been initialized using **s_init_lock**. **s_lock** is always successful; it spins as long as is necessary to acquire the lock. **s_clock** is successful only if the lock is free; if the lock is held by another process, **s_clock** returns the value L_FAILED. **s_clock** can be used when a process does not need to acquire a particular lock (for instance, when another lock could be used instead).

s_unlock unlocks the lock whose address is **lp**.

S_INIT_LOCK, S_LOCK, S_UNLOCK, and S_CLOCK are C-preprocessor macros. These macros are found in the header file */usr/include/parallel/parallel.h*. The macros are faster than the normal function calls, but they can add to the code size. See the source code in *<parallel/parallel.h>* for more information on the C macros.

SEE ALSO

intro(3PPS), shmalloc(3PPS), fortran(1), ld(1),   *Guide to Parallel Programming*

NOTES

The function names **s_init_lock**, **s_lock**, **s_clock**, and **s_unlock** are used in C, C++, Pascal, and FORTRAN. In C and C++, the **lp** argument is passed as a pointer to the lock, while in Pascal and FORTRAN, the argument is the address of the lock itself.

NAME

s_init_barrier, s_wait_barrier – initialize barrier, wait at barrier

SYNOPSIS

C syntax:

#include <parallel/parallel.h>
s_init_barrier (bp, nprocs)
sbarrier_t *bp;
int nprocs;

S_INIT_BARRIER (bp, nprocs)

s_wait_barrier (bp)
sbarrier_t *bp;

S_WAIT_BARRIER (bp)

C++ syntax:

#include <parallel/parallel.h>
extern "C" s_init_barrier (sbarrier_t *bp, int nprocs)
extern "C" s_wait_barrier (sbarrier_t *bp)

Pascal syntax

import ParallelMultitasking;
          or
procedure s_init_barrier (var barrier:sbarrier_t; nprocs:integer); external;
procedure s_wait_barrier (var barrier:sbarrier_t); external;

FORTRAN syntax

integer*4 barrier, nprocs
subroutine s_init_barrier (barrier, nprocs)
subroutine s_wait_barrier (barrier)

DESCRIPTION

s_init_barrier initializes a barrier as a rendezvous point for exactly **nprocs** processes. This barrier can be used subsequently with **s_wait_barrier** .

In C and C++, a barrier is a shared data structure of type sbarrier_t. In Pascal, a barrier is a record. In FORTRAN, a barrier is an INTEGER*4 variable. When compiling Pascal and FORTRAN programs, you must specify the **–mp** option to place the barrier into shared memory.

s_wait_barrier delays the process in a busy wait until exactly **nprocs** processes have called **s_wait_barrier**. At that point, all processes exit the busy wait simultaneously. The barrier must have been previously initialized using **s_init_barrier** .

Results are undefined if more than **nprocs** processes call **s_wait_barrier**. A barrier can be used any number of times without being re-initialized. A barrier should not be re-initialized while processes are waiting at the barrier.

S_INIT_BARRIER and S_WAIT_BARRIER are C-preprocessor macros. These macros are found in the header file */usr/include/parallel/parallel.h*. When compiled in line, the macros are faster than the normal function calls, but they can add to the code size. See the source code in *<parallel/parallel.h>* for more information on the macros.

SEE ALSO
> intro(3PPS), shmalloc(3PPS) *Guide to Parallel Programming*

NAME

shbrk, shsbrk – change shared data segment size

SYNOPSIS

C syntax:

#include <parallel/parallel.h>
caddr_t shbrk(addr)
caddr_t addr;

char * caddr_t shsbrk(incr)
int incr;

C++ syntax:

#include <parallel/parallel.h>
extern "C" caddr_t shbrk(caddr_t addr)

extern "C" caddr_t shsbrk(int incr)

Pascal syntax

import ParallelStorage;
            or
function shbrk(addr : pointer) : pointer; external;
function shsbrk(incr : integer) : pointer; external;

FORTRAN syntax

DESCRIPTION

For a set of parallel processes executing a single application, **shbrk** sets the
system's idea of the lowest shared data segment location not used by the program (called the shared break) to **addr** (rounded up to the next multiple of the
system's page size). Locations greater than **addr** and below the stack pointer
or another memory mapped region (see **mmap**(2SEQ)) are not in the address
space and will thus cause a memory violation if accessed.

In the alternate function, **shsbrk, incr** more bytes are added to the program's
shared data space and a pointer to the start of the new area is returned.

When a program begins execution via **execve**, the shared break is set at the
highest location defined by the program. Ordinarily, therefore, only programs
with growing shared data areas need to use **shsbrk**.

When **shbrk** and **shsbrk** increase a program's address space, they also
attempt to increase its allowable resident set size (see **vm_ctl**(2SEQ)).

ERRORS

Zero is returned if the shared break could be set; –1 if the program requests
more memory than the system limit. **shsbrk** returns –1 if the break could not
be set.

shbrk and **shsbrk** fails and no additional memory is allocated if any of the
following error conditions occur:

[EINVAL]   The shared break address would be lowered.

[ENOMEM]   The routine cannot allocate file system space to expand the
                    file which has been memory mapped to the shared data seg-
                    ment (see **mmap**(2SEQ)). The routine tries to allocate file
                    system space from directories in the following order:

                    1. the directory indicated by the **TMPPATH** environment vari-
                    able
                    2. the current directory
                    3. the user's home directory
                    4. the directory */usr/tmp*
                    5. the directory */tmp*

[ENOMEM]   The new shared data segment would overlap the stack seg-
                    ment.

SEE ALSO

execve(2), shmalloc(3PPS), end(3), vm_ctl(2SEQ), mmap(2SEQ) , *Guide to Parallel Programming*

BUGS

At this time, the size of the shared data segment can only be increased.

The shared break cannot be set above the stack segment limit for any of the
processes in the program. (Remember that each process can have a different
stack size.) If a process sets the shared break above the bottom of any process's stack, any reference to the overlapping area of that stack causes a core
dump and aborts the program with a status of SIGSEGV.

shbrk and **shsbrk** use the SIGSEGV signal and signal handler for internal
purposes. Users who declare their own SIGSEGV handler cannot expect reliable results from these routines.

If a **shbrk** or **shsbrk** call causes the shared data segment to overlap a memory mapped region, the shared data segment replaces the mapped region.

NAME

shmalloc, shrealloc, shfree – shared memory allocator

SYNOPSIS

C syntax:

char *shmalloc(size)
unsigned size;
shfree(ptr)
char *ptr;

char *shrealloc(ptr,size)
char *ptr;
unsigned size;

C++ syntax:

#include <parallel/parallel.h>
extern "C" char *shmalloc(unsigned size)
extern "C" shfree(char *ptr)

extern "C" char *shrealloc(char *ptr, unsigned size)

Pascal syntax

import ParallelStorage;
                or
function shmalloc(size : integer) : pointer; external;
function shrealloc(ptr : pointer; size : integer) : pointer; external;
procedure shfree(ptr : pointer); external;

FORTRAN syntax

DESCRIPTION

shmalloc, shrealloc, and **shfree** provide a simple general-purpose shared memory allocation package for a set of processes executing a single application. To use these routines, the program must have been linked with the parallel-programming library (*libpps.a*) and *libseq.a*. **shmalloc** returns a pointer to a block of at least **size** bytes beginning on a 4-byte word boundary.

The argument to **shfree** is a pointer to a block previously allocated by **shmalloc**; this space is made available for further allocation, but its contents are left undisturbed.

Grave disorder results if the space assigned by **shmalloc** is overrun or if some random number is handed to **shfree**.

shmalloc maintains multiple lists of free blocks according to size, allocating space from the appropriate list. It calls **shsbrk** (see **shbrk**(3PPS)) to get more memory from the system when there is no suitable space already free. **shmalloc** and **shfree** coordinate the allocation of shared memory among the processes in the task. They maintain a consistent list of free blocks even when several processes are allocating shared memory concurrently. Concurrent requests for shared memory blocks always return unique blocks from the program's shared data segment.

shrealloc changes the size of the block pointed to by **ptr** to **size** bytes and returns a pointer to the (possibly moved) block. The contents will be unchanged up to the lesser of the new and old sizes. If **ptr** points to a freed block, **shrealloc** returns NULL.

When any of these allocation routines increases a program's address space, it also attempts to increase its allowable resident set size (see **vm_ctl**(2SEQ)).

DIAGNOSTICS

shmalloc returns a NULL pointer (0) if there is no available shared memory or if the region has been detectably corrupted by storing data outside the bounds of a block. **shmalloc** may be recompiled to check the arena very stringently on every transaction; those sites with a source code license may check the source code to see how this can be done.

SEE ALSO

shbrk(3PPS), vm_ctl(2SEQ), *Guide to Parallel Programming*

Appendix C
Parallel Programming under DYNIX

Appendix C
Parallel Programming under DYNIX

This appendix describes the differences between the DYNIX and DYNIX/ptx operating systems that affect parallel programming.

C.1 Manuals Sets

The manual sets for DYNIX and DYNIX/ptx are unique to each operating system. Table C-1 lists the DYNIX/ptx manuals referenced in this guide and identifies the equivalent manual under DYNIX.

Table C-1
Manual Titles

DYNIX/ptx Title	DYNIX Title
DYNIX/ptx Reference Manual	DYNIX Programmer's Manual
DYNIX/ptx C User's Manual	ATS C User's Manual
ptx/FORTRAN User's Manual	ATS FORTRAN User's Manual
ptx/C++ Release Notes	DYNIX C++ Release Notes
ptx/PASCAL Release Notes and EPC Pascal-E User's Manual	Pascal Compiler User's Manual
DYNIX/ptx System Configuration and Performance Guide	Building DYNIX Systems with Config in the DYNIX Programmer's Manual

Man page section numbers also differ between DYNIX and DYNIX/ptx. Table C-2 lists the DYNIX/ptx man page section numbers and the DYNIX equivalent.

Table C-2
Man Page Section Numbers

Description	DYNIX/ptx Section No.	DYNIX Section No.
Commands	1	same
System Calls	2	2
Sequent-specific system calls	2SEQ	2
C library routines	3C	same
Math library routines	3M	same
Networking Support Utilities	3N	same
Parallel-programming library routines	3PPS	3P
Standard I/O Library Routines	3S	same
Sequent-specific I/O Library Routines	3SEQ	3
Special Routines	3X	same
File Formats	4	5
Miscellaneous facilities	5	7
Special Files	7	4
Stand-alone utilities	8	same

C.2 Parallel-Programming Tools

DYNIX supports several additional tools that you can use to develop or run parallel programs under DYNIX/ptx. These tools are described in the following paragraphs.

C.2.1 The apply Utility

With DYNIX, in addition to the parallel support embedded in the **sh, lint,** and **make** commands, you can use the **apply** command to execute system commands in parallel. When you specify the –P*n* option on the **apply** command line, **apply** runs *n* commands concurrently. If you do not specify the –P*n* option and the **PARALLEL** environment variable is defined, **apply** uses the value specified by **PARALLEL** for *n*. If **PARALLEL** is not defined, *n* defaults to a value of 1. For example, the following command compares two sets of files in parallel and writes the results of both comparisons to the file *diff.log*.

```
apply –P2 –3 diff –bcl matmul.f matmul2.f –bcl xlf xla.f > diff.log
```

For more information on **apply**, refer to the **apply**(1) man page.

C.2.2 The gprof Utility

Under DYNIX, you can use the **gprof** utility as well as the **prof** utility to determine which subprograms (subroutines or functions) account for most of a program's execution time. The **gprof** utility provides more detailed information than **prof** and is generally considered more useful.

The steps to create a **gprof** listing are the same as those to create a **prof** listing, except for the following differences:

- You must specify the –**pg** compiler option instead of the –**p** compiler option.

- You must use the **gprof** command instead of the **prof** command

Note that profile data is written to a file called *gmon.out* and that entering the **gprof** command produces an ASCII file named *gmon.sum*, which contains the program execution profile.

In addition to the subprogram list **gprof** produces a set of call graphs. Figure C-1 shows a subprogram call graph.

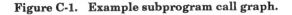

```
                 9.36   0.00    5174/133874      sgesl [6]
               232.88   0.00  128700/133874      sgefa [3]
  [4]   83.7  242.24   0.00  133874             saxpy [4]
```

Figure C-1. Example subprogram call graph.

The following information in the call graph should be reviewed:

- The leftmost column contains the index of the call graph. The call graphs cross-reference each other by their index numbers.

- The second column contains the percentage of the total program execution time accounted for by this subprogram and its descendents (the subprograms that it calls). Figure C-1 shows that the subprogram accounts for 83.7% of the total execution time.

- The last column lists the subprogram, its ancestors, and its descendents. The name that stands out to the left is the subprogram that is the subject of the graph; in Figure C-1, the subprogram is saxpy. The names listed above this line are the subprogram's ancestors, and the names listed below are its descendent. The square brackets following each subprogram name contain that subprogram's index number.

From Figure C-1 you can see that the routine saxpy is called by two routines, sgefa and sgesl. You will start by looking at these routines and working outwards through the routines in their call graphs until you find the outermost loop, then working back inward through the loops until you find one to execute in parallel.

The information presented here should enable you to use **gprof** to analyze a program for parallel execution. For more detailed information on **gprof**, refer to the DYNIX man page **gprof**(1) or to the article "gprof: A Call Graph Execution Profiler." Both the man page and the article are in the *DYNIX Programmer's Manual.*

C.2.3 The Profiling Library

You can monitor execution of parallel programs that use the parallel-programming library by linking in the profiling version of the library, *lpps_p.a*. To link in this library, you must compile the source files with the –**pg** compiler option and specify the –**p** option at link time. When the program is run, it produces a file with the suffix *.mon* for the parent process and each child process created by the program. You can then use the **prof** profiling utility to create an execution profile for each process, or you can use the utility's –**s** option to concatenate the *.mon* files and create an execution profile that includes the parent and child processes and all calls to parallel-programming library routines.

For more information on the –**pg** and –**p** compiler options, refer to the **cc**(1), **fortran**(1), and **pascal** man pages. For more information on the **prof** utility, refer to the man page **prof**(1) in the *DYNIX Programmer's Manual*.

C.3 Compiling Your C Programs

When compiling your C programs under DYNIX, you do not need to precede Sequent-specific options with the –**Wc** flag.

C.4 Input/Output

This section describes the differences in I/O between DYNIX and DYNIX/ptx that can affect parallel programs. These differences are as follows:

- Buffering of I/O
- The **fcntl**() system call

C.4.1 Buffering of I/O

Under DYNIX, standard I/O is buffered, so you must evaluate carefully where to place calls to I/O routines in your parallel program. For example, consider the following C program:

```
#include <stdio.h>

main()
{
    void worker();
    printf("Hello ");
    m_fork(worker);
    m_kill_procs();
}
void worker()
{
    printf("world ");
}
```

Assume the source code exists in the file *hello.c* and the program is compiled and linked using the following command:

cc hello.c –lpps –lseq

Executing *a.out* produces the following output on a four-processor system.

```
Hello world Hello world Hello world Hello world
```

Since the buffer contained the string "Hello " before the call to **m_fork**(), each child process has a copy of the *stdio* buffer which includes the string "Hello ". To clear the *stdio* buffer, call **fflush**() before calling **m_fork**(). The program now looks like this:

```
#include <stdio.h>

main()
{
    void worker();
    printf("Hello ");
    fflush(stdout);
    mfork(worker);
    m_kill_procs();
}
void worker()
{
    printf("world ");
}
```

Executing this version of the program on the same system would produce the following output:

```
Hello world world world world
```

C.4.2 The fcntl() System Call

The **fcntl** system call is still available under DYNIX, but you must use the FAPPEND flag (not the O_APPEND flag) to ensure that each write occurs at the end of the file.

C.5 Signals

Under DYNIX, use the **signal**(3C) routine to manage signals. The **sigact**()
and **sigaction**() routines are supported under DYNIX/ptx only.

C.6 Memory Management and System Configuration

Under DYNIX, if you are using the C shell, you can use the **limit** command
to display the default value of *_stack_limit*, the size of the shared stack.

If your system is not configured to allow you to change your virtual memory
parameters, the file to edit to set the appropriate parameters is
/sys/conf/param.c. Once set, you can use the DYNIX **config** utility to
reconfigure the system.

You can also display and set a per-process limit to your resident set size
using the **getrlimit**() and **setrlimit**() routines, respectively.

C.7 Synchronization and IPC

Under the DYNIX operating system support for asynchronous parallel
programming is provided through standard UNIX 4.2BSD system calls, with
special DYNIX system calls and libraries, and with system calls in the
System V Applications Environment (SVAE).

The System V Applications Environment includes a set of system calls for
setting up and manipulating message queues and counting, blocking
semaphores. These system calls have been added to the standard DYNIX C
library, and are transparently available to programs linked in either the ucb
(default) universe or the att universe. Other system calls that are specific
to the System V Applications Environment are available only if the System V
Applications Environment is installed, and only to programs linked in the
att universe. See the *DYNIX SVAE Summary* for details. (The programs
and code samples shown in Appendix A of this manual are designed to be
compiled and linked in the ucb universe.)

The UNIX IPC Facility

The Interprocess Communication (IPC) subsystem of UNIX 4.2bsd provides the ability to transfer data directly between processes using system calls such as **read**() and **write**(). The unidirectional **pipe** facility found in all versions of UNIX is one application of the UNIX 4.2bsd IPC facilities. Other applications use bidirectional data connections or broadcast packets of data to a group of processes. For more information on the IPC facilities, refer to the article "A 4.2BSD Interprocess Communication Primer" in Volume 2 of the *DYNIX/ptx Programmer's Manual*, and to man pages such as **socket**(2), **bind**(2), **listen**(2), **connect**(2), and **accept**(2).

On Sequent systems, interprocess communication can often be accomplished more easily and efficiently using shared memory. However, the IPC facilities are extremely useful for certain types of applications, and can be used in situations where shared memory cannot—for example, in applications that may involve processes on different systems.

System V Support

The **msgsnd**(), **msgrcv**(), **msgget**(), and **msgctl**() system calls from the System V Applications Environment provide a mechanism for sending and receiving data between processes via message queues. Data can be packaged in messages of arbitrary length. For specifications of these system calls, refer to the **msgop**(2), **msgget**(2), and **msgctl**(2) entries in AT&T's *UNIX System V Programmer Reference Manual*.

Bibliography

The area of parallel programming is extremely well published. An attempt to create a thorough bibliography of the subject is beyond the scope of this document. Therefore, the following sections provide a sampling of literature on parallel programming, parallel programming languages, and parallel programming algorithms and methods. Many of the works listed here contain extensive bibliographies, which should enable you to find further information on topics of special interest to you.

General Topics in Parallel Programming

1. Baer, J.L. "A Survey of Some Theoretical Aspects of Multiprocessing." *Computing Surveys*, Vol. 5 No. 1, March 1973, pp. 31-80.

2. Beck, R., and D. M. Olien. "A Parallel-Programming Process Model." *IEEE Software*, Vol. 6, No. 3, May 1989, pp. 63-72.

3. Bowen, B.A., and R.J.A. Buhr. *The Logical Design of Multiple-Microprocessor Systems*. Englewood Cliffs, N.J.: Prentice-Hall, Inc., 1980.

4. Dinning, A. "A Survey of Synchronization Methods for Parallel Computers." *Computer*, Vol. 22, No. 7, July 1989, pp. 66-77.

5. Dubois, M., and C. Scheurich. "Synchronization, Coherence, and Event Ordering in Multiprocessors." *Computer*, Vol. 21, No. 2, February 1988, pp. 9-21.

6. Duncan, R. "A Survey of Parallel Computer Architectures." *Computer*, Vol. 23, No. 2, February 1990, pp. 5-16.

7. Gelernter, D. "Domesticating Parallelism." *Computer*, Vol. 19, No. 8, August 1986, pp. 12-16.

8. Gonzalez, M.J., and C.V. Ramamoorthy. "Parallel Task Execution in a Decentralized System." *IEEE Transactions on Computers*, Vol. 21, No. 12, December 1972, pp. 1310-1322.

9. Graunke, G., and S. Thakkar. "Synchronization Algorithms for Shared-Memory Multiprocessors." *Computer*, Vol. 23, No. 6, June 1990, pp. 60-69.

10. Hockney, R.W., and C.R. Jesshope. *Parallel Computers*. Bristol, England: Adam Hilger Ltd., 1981.

11. Hudak, P. "Para-Functional Programming." *Computer*, Vol. 19, No. 8, August 1986, pp. 61-71.

12. Hudak, P. "Exploring Parafunctional Programming: Separating the What from the How." *IEEE Software*, Vol. 5, No. 1, January 1988, pp. 54-61.

13. Hwang, K., and F.A. Briggs. *Computer Architecture and Parallel Processing*. New York: McGraw-Hill Book Co., 1984.

14. Kowalik, J.S., ed. *Parallel MIMD Computation: The HEP Supercomputer and Its Applications*. Cambridge, Mass.: MIT Press, 1985.

15. Kuck, D.J. "A Survey of Parallel Machine Organization and Programming." *Computing Surveys*, Vol. 9, No. 1, March 1977, pp. 29-59.

16. Kuck, D.J. *The Structure of Computers and Computations*. New York: John Wiley & Sons, Inc., 1978.

17. Lampson, B.W., M. Paul, and H.J. Siegert, eds. *Distributed Systems - Architecture and Implementation* in Goos, G. and J. Hartmanis, eds. *Lecture Notes in Computer Science* Berlin and Heidelberg, W. Germany: Springer-Verlag, 1981.

18. Lorin, H. *Parallelism in Hardware and Software: Real and Apparent Concurrency*. Englewood Cliffs, N.J.: Prentice-Hall, Inc., 1972.

19. Lovett, T., and S. Thakkar. "The Symmetry Multiprocessor System." *Proceedings of the 1988 International Conference on Parallel Processing*, Vol. 1, pp. 303-310.

20. Polychronopoulos, C.D., and D.J. Kuck. "Guided Self-Scheduling: A Practical Scheduling Scheme for Parallel Supercomputers." *IEEE Transactions on Computers*, Vol. C-36, No. 12, December 1987, pp. 1425-1437.

21. Polychronopoulos, Constantine D. "The Impact of Run-Time Overhead on Usable Parallelism." *Proceedings of the 1988 International Conference on Parallel Processing*, Vol. 1, pp. 108-112.

22. Porterfield, A. "Software Methods for Improvement of Cache Performance on Supercomputer Applications." Rice University Technical Report TR90-93, May 1989.

23. Rodrigue, G. (ed.). *Parallel Computations*. New York: Academic Press, 1982.

24. Shani, S. "Scheduling Multipipeline and Multiprocessor Computers." *IEEE Transactions on Computers*, Vol. 33, No. 7, July, 1984, pp. 637-645.

25. Stenstrom, P. "Reducing Contention in Shared-Memory Multiprocessors." *Computer*, Vol. 21, No. 11, Nov. 1988, pp. 26-37.

26. Thakkar, S. et al. "New Directions in Scalable Shared-Memory Multiprocessor Architectures." *Computer*, Vol. 23, No. 6, June 1990, pp. 71-83.

Parallel Programming Languages

1. Appelbe, W.F., and C.E. McDowell. "High-level Language Primitives for Parallel Algorithms." Internal Report, Electrical Engineering and Computer Science Dept. C-014, University of California, San Diego, March 1985.

2. Beck, B. "Shared-Memory Parallel Programming in C++." *IEEE Software*, Vol. 7, No. 4, July 1990. pp. 38-48.

3. Brooks, E.D. "A Multitasking Kernel for the C and FORTRAN Programming Languages." *Technical Report UCID-20167*, Lawrence Livermore National Laboratory, September 1984.

4. Carriero, N., and D. Gelernter. "Linda in Context." *Communications of the ACM*, Vol. 32, No. 4, April 1989, pp. 444-458.

5. Gehani, A. H., and W. D. Roome. "Concurrent C -- An Overview" *Conference Proceedings* Winter USENIX, 1985.

6. Gehani, N. *Ada Concurrent Programming*. Englewood Cliffs, N.J.: Prentice-Hall, Inc., 1984. [Gehani 1984]

7. Halstead, R., and J. Loaiza. "Multilisp: A Language for Concurrent Symbolic Computation." *ACM Transactions on Programming Languages and Systems*, October 1985.

8. Hansen, P. B. *The Architecture of Concurrent Programs*. Englewood Cliffs, N.J.: Prentice-Hall, Inc., 1977.

9. Mundie, D.A., and D.A. Fischer. "Parallel Processing in Ada." *Computer*, Vol. 19, No. 8, August 1986, pp. 20-25.

10. Oldehoeft, R., and D. C. Cann. "Applicative Parallelism on a Shared-Memory Multiprocessor." *IEEE Software*, Vol. 5, No. 1, January 1988, pp. 62-70.

11. Padua, D.A., D.J. Kuck, and D.H. Lawrie. "High-Speed Multiprocessors and Compilation Techniques." *IEEE Transactions on Computers*, Vol. 29, No. 9, September 1980, pp. 763-776.

12. Shapiro, E. "A Subset of Concurrent Prolog and Its Interpreter." *ICOT Technical Report TR-003*, February 1983.

13. United States Department of Defense. *Reference Manual for the Ada Programming Language.* ANSI/MIL-STD-1815A-1983, February 1983.

14. Wolfe, M.J. "Multiprocessor Synchronization for Concurrent Loops." *IEEE Software* Vol. 5, No. 1, January 1988, pp. 34-42.

15. Wolfe, M.J. *Optimizing Supercompilers for Supercomputers.* Cambridge, Massachusetts: The MIT Press, 1989.

Algorithms and Programming Techniques

1. Anderson, T.E. "The Performance of Spin Lock Alternatives for Shared-Memory Multiprocessors" *IEEE Transactions on Parallel and Distributed Systems*, Vol. 1, No. 1, January 1990, pp. 6-16.

2. Andrews, G., and F. Schneider. "Concepts and Notations for Concurrent Programming." *ACM Computing Surveys*, Vol. 15, No. 1, March 1983, pp. 3-44.

3. Banerjee, U., S.C. Shen, D.J. Kuck, and R.A. Towle. "Time and Parallel Processor Bounds for FORTRAN-like Loops." *IEEE Transactions on Computers*, Vol. 28, No. 9, September 1979, pp. 660-670.

4. Banerjee, U., and D.D. Gajski. "Fast Execution of Loops with IF Statements." *IEEE Transactions on Computers*, Vol. 33, No. 11, November 1984, pp. 1030-1033.

5. Bernstein, A.J. "Analysis of Programs for Parallel Processing." *IEEE Transactions on Electronic Computers*, Vol. 15, No. 5, October 1966, pp. 757-763.

6. Cray Research, Inc. "Multitasking User Guide" *Cray Computer Systems Technical Note SN-0222*. Mendota Heights, Minn.: Cray Research, Inc., 1984.

7. Cytron, R. "Useful Parallelism in a Multiprocessing Environment." *Proceedings of the International Conference on Parallel Processing.* Washington, D.C.: IEEE Computer Society Press, 1985. pp. 450-457.

8. Gajski, D.D. "An Algorithm for Solving Linear Recurrence Systems on Parallel and Pipelined Machines." *IEEE Transactions on Computers,* Vol. 30, No. 3, March 1981, pp. 190-206.

9. Hansen, P. B. "Concurrent Programming Concepts." *ACM Computing Surveys,* Vol. 5, No. 4, December 1973, pp. 223-245.

10. Hoare, C.A.R. "Communicating Sequential Processes." *Proceedings of the ACM,* Vol. 21, No. 11, August 1978, pp. 666-667.

11. Kasahara, H., and S. Narita. "Practical Multiprocessor Scheduling Algorithms for Efficient Parallel Processing." *IEEE Transactions on Computers,* Vol. 33, No. 11, November 1984, pp. 1023-1029.

12. Kennedy, K., and D. Callahan. "Analysis of Interprocedural Side Effects in a Parallel Programming Environment". Department of Computer Science, Rice University, Houston, Texas, May 1987.

13. Knuth, D. "An Empirical Study of FORTRAN Programs." *Software Practice and Experience,* Vol. 1, 1971, pp. 105-133.

14. Kuck, D.J., Y. Muraoka, and S.C. Chen. "On the Number of Operations Simultaneously Executable in FORTRAN-like Programs and Their Resulting Speed-up." *IEEE Transactions on Computers,* Vol. 21 No. 12, December 1972, pp. 1293-1310.

15. Lusk, E.L., R. Olson, and R.A. Overbeek. "A Tutorial on the Use of Monitors in C: Writing Portable Code for Multiprocessors". Mathematics and Computer Science Division, Argonne National Laboratory, Argonne, Ill., 1986.

16. Maruyama, K. "On the Parallel Evaluation of Polynomials." *IEEE Transactions on Computers,* Vol. 22, No. 1, January 1973, pp. 2-5.

17. Mehrotra, R., and E.F. Gehringer. "Superlinear Speedup Through Randomized Algorithms." *Proceedings of the International Conference on Parallel Processing,* Washington, D.C.: IEEE Computer Society Press, 1985. pp. 291-300.

18. Muchnick, S.S., and N.D. Jones, eds. *Program Flow Analysis: Theory and Applications.* Englewood Cliffs, N.J.: Prentice-Hall, Inc., 1981.

19. Padua, D.A., and M.J. Wolfe. "Advanced Compiler Optimization f or Supercomputers." *Communications of the ACM*, Vol. 29, No. 12, December 1986, pp. 1184-1201.

20. Quinn, M. J. *Designing Efficient Algorithms for Parallel Computers.* New York: McGraw-Hill Book Co., 1987.

21. Paige, R.C., and C.P. Kruskal. "Parallel Algorithms for Shortest Path Problems." *Proceedings of the International Conference on Parallel Processing*, Washington, D.C.: IEEE Computer Society Press, 1985, pp. 14-19.

22. Ramamoorthy, C.V., and M.J. Gonzalez. "A Survey of the Techniques for Recognizing Parallel Processable Streams in Computer Programs." *AFIPS Conference Proceedings, 1969 Fall Joint Computer Conference* Montvale, N.J.: AFIPS Press, 1969, pp. 1-15.

23. Riseman, E.M., and C.C. Foster. "The Inhibition of Potential Parallelism by Conditional Jumps." *IEEE Transactions on Computers*, Vol. 21, No. 12, December 1972, pp. 1405-1411.

24. Rudolph, L., and W. Steiger. "Subset Selection in Parallel." *Proceedings of the International Conference on Parallel Processing*, Washington, D.C.: IEEE Computer Society Press, 1985, pp. 11-13.

25. Tenorio, M.F.M., and D.I. Moldovan. "Mapping Production Systems into Multiprocessors." *Proceedings of the International Conference on Parallel Processing* , Washington, D.C.: IEEE Computer Society Press, 1985, pp. 56-62.

26. Tjaden, G.S., and M.J. Flynn. "Detection and Parallel Execution of Independent Instructions." *IEEE Transactions on Computers*, Vol. 19, No. 10, October 1970, pp. 889-895.

27. Wei, M.C., and H.A. Sholl. "An Expression Model for Extraction and Evaluation of Parallelism in Control Structures." *IEEE Transactions on Computers*, Vol. 31, No. 9, September 1982, pp. 851-863.

28. Wolfe, M.J. "Techniques for Improving the Inherent Parallelism in Programs." *Technical Report UIUCDCS-R-78-929, Department of Computer Science, University of Illinois*, July 1978.

Glossary

Aging. Refers to the adjustment of a process's priority based on the time it has spent executing.

Antidependence. A type of data dependence in which one operation *reads* a memory location that is written by a subsequent operation.

Array processor. A machine that contains multiple functional units and uses pipelining to improve performance on vector operations.

Atomic. Indivisible.

Barrier. A synchronization point. All processes wait at the barrier until the last process arrives, at which time all processes proceed.

Blocking. Releasing a processor for use by other processes. Processes can choose to block, rather than spin, during long periods of inactivity.

Busy-waiting. See **Spinning**.

Cache. A random-access high-speed memory used as a buffer between a processor and main memory. Every processor on a Symmetry system has its own cache. A cache is designed to anticipate which instructions the processor will need and store these instructions so that the processor doesn't have to access main memory for each instruction. Use of a cache improves overall system performance by reducing traffic on the system bus.

Child (process). See **Fork**.

Control dependence. One of two classes of program dependence. A control dependence relation exists between two statements when the execution of one is dependent on the result of a test in the first.

Critical section. A program section that can yield incorrect results if two or more processes try to execute the section at the same time.

Data dependence. One of two classes of program dependence. Data dependence relations exist when the value of one data depends on the other for correct results. If a data dependency exists, the statements containing those values cannot execute in parallel. The three types of data dependence are flow dependence, antidependence, and output dependence.

Data partitioning. A programming method that involves creating multiple, identical processes, each of which performs the same operations on a different portion of the program data.

Dependence theory (program). Defines how, in order to guarantee correct results, some program operations depend on previous operations. Once all the dependence relations are identified, the ordering necessary to guarantee correct results has also been defined. There are two classes of program dependence: **data dependence** and **control dependence**.

Dependent loop. A loop in which the operations in each iteration depend on the results of previous iterations.

Dynamic scheduling. A scheduling method that allows processes to schedule their own tasks through a shared task queue or shared counter.

DYNIX. "DYnamic uNIX," an operating system for Sequent Symmetry systems. DYNIX is a version of UNIX 4.2BSD that has been modified to support both software-transparent multiprocessing and explicit parallel programming.

DYNIX/ptx. A operating system for Sequent Symmetry systems. DYNIX/ptx is compatible with AT&T UNIX System V Release 3.2 (SVID Issue 3 compliant) and conforms to the *IEEE Standard 1003.1-1988 Portable Operating System Interface for Computer Environments* (POSIX).

Event. Something that must happen before a task or process can proceed.

Flow dependence. A type of data dependence in which one operation sets a data value that is used by ("flows to") a subsequent operation.

Fork. A system call that creates a new process which is identical to the calling process. The calling process is called the "parent", and the new process is called the "child."

Function partitioning. A programming method that involves creating multiple processes (usually running different programs) and having them perform different operations on a shared data set.

Heap. The portion of a program's data area that is allocated at run time.

Heterogeneous multitasking. See **Function partitioning.**

Granularity. Refers to the level of parallelism, which can be at the module, statement or instruction level.

Homogeneous multitasking. See **Data partitioning.**

Independent loop. A loop that passes no information between loop iterations other than the value of the loop index.

Local data. Refers to the scope of the name that identifies a data object. Data is local to a function when that function contains a definition for that data object. A data object with the same name in a different function is local to that function only. Use "private data" to refer to data that is accessible by only one process.

Lock. A semaphore which ensures that only one process at a time can access a shared data structure or execute a critical region of code.

Microtasking. A data-partitioning method that automatically divides the computing load according to the number of available processes.

Multicomputer. A multiple CPU computer system with distributed memory.

Multiprogramming. An operating system feature that allows a computer to execute multiple unrelated programs concurrently.

Multitasking. A programming technique that allows a single application to consist of multiple processes executing tasks concurrently.

Mutual exclusion. Two events are mutually exclusive when they cannot occur at the same time.

Ordered critical section. A point in a program where a task depends on the results of a previous task and execution cannot proceed until the previous task is finished.

Output dependence. A type of data dependence in which one operation *writes* a value in a memory location and that same memory location is used to write a value in a subsequent operation.

Overhead (program). Time and computation not spent in calculating the result of a program. Some examples of overhead are data initialization, I/O, and synchronization.

Parent (process). See **Fork**.

Post. One or more processes wait for an event until another process posts the event.

Private data. Data that is accessible by only one process.

Process. An instruction stream. Different processes may be instances of the same program, as when the **vi** editor is used by several people simultaneously. Because of DYNIX/ptx's dynamic load balancing, a process may migrate from one CPU to another during its lifetime.

Process identification number (PID). A number that uniquely identifies a process.

Scheduling. Dividing computing tasks among processes.

Semaphore. A shared data structure used to synchronize the actions of multiple cooperating processes.

Shared data. Data that is accessible by more than one process.

Spinning. Waiting for a resource or an event by running a loop that does nothing except check the availability of that resource or the status of an event. Spinning avoids the overhead associated with task switching.

Static scheduling. A scheduling method that assigns tasks to processes at run time in a predetermined fashion. For example, a statically scheduled data-partitioning program might divide loop iterations evenly among processes.

Superuser. A privileged user who owns most system files and uses the login **root**. The superuser can access any file, regardless of its permission levels, and performs most system administration tasks.

Tightly coupled. Describes a system in which all processors share a single pool of memory.

True dependence. See **Flow dependence.**

Index

C

I-J-K

L

M

U

V-W-X-Y-Z

Other Sequent publications for programmers:

DYNIX/ptx Reference Manual

DYNIX/ptx Programming Tools Guide

DYNIX/ptx C and Language Tools Binder:
  C User's Manual
  ld User's Guide
  lint Reference Manual
  Assembly Language User's Manual
  Pdbx User's Manual
  Man Pages

ptx/FORTRAN Binder:
  ptx/FORTRAN User's Manual
  Man Pages

ptx/PASCAL Release Notes and *EPC Pascal-E User's Manual*

ptx/C++ Release Notes

About Sequent

Sequent Computer Systems, Inc. is an established industry leader in delivering parallel processing computing systems for business and research applications. Sequent announced the first commercially viable parallel processing computer, the Balance 8000, in September, 1984. Since then, Sequent has introduced a full spectrum of microprocessor-based binary-compatible parallel processing systems that span a performance range from deskside to mainframe. In January of 1991, Sequent introduced its newest generation systems, the Symmetry 2000, which incorporate 486^{TM} based technology, extending Symmetry's industry-leading price performance.

Sequent's open architectured systems combine the ease of use of the standard UNIX® operating system with the performance advantages of multiple tightly-coupled 32-bit microprocessors, each offering supermini performance. DYNIX/ptx®, Sequent's implementation of UNIX, runs AT&T's System V interface environment. In multi-user applications, DYNIX/ptx makes the parallel processing architecture completely transparent to existing user software, automatically balancing loads across multiple processors. C, C++, COBOL, Pascal, and FORTRAN compilers, programming tools, communications and networking software, and PC interface software are available. Sequent's extensive third party software program, LINKS, includes the leading relational database management systems, office automation software, numerous spreadsheet programs, cross-development tools, and a variety of other utilities.